Withdrawn from stock

Date 27/6/25

Reason No longer used

DANIEL CRAIG

First published in
Great Britain in 2007
by A Jot Publishing

UK address:
suite 774, 28 Old Brompton Rd
London SW7 3SS

© A Jot Publishing
All rights reserved. No part
of this publication may be
reproduced, stored in or
introduced into a retrieval
system, or transmitted in any
form or by any means (electronic,
mechanical, photocopying, recording
or otherwise) without the prior
written permission of both the
copyright owner and the
publisher of this book.

ISBN: 978-1-905904-50-1

Design: Jay Huggins
Daniel Craig Photographs: Rex Features

DANIEL CRAIG

Brandon Hurst

007
CASINO ROYALE
MUNICH
ENDURING LOVE
LOVE IS THE DEVIL
LARA CROFT TOMB RAIDER
Il film più spettacolare del nuovo millennio
L4YER CAKE
ROAD TO PERDITION
MUNICH
CASINO ROYALE
NOVEMBER 17
ADRIEN BRODY · KEIRA KNIGHTLEY
007

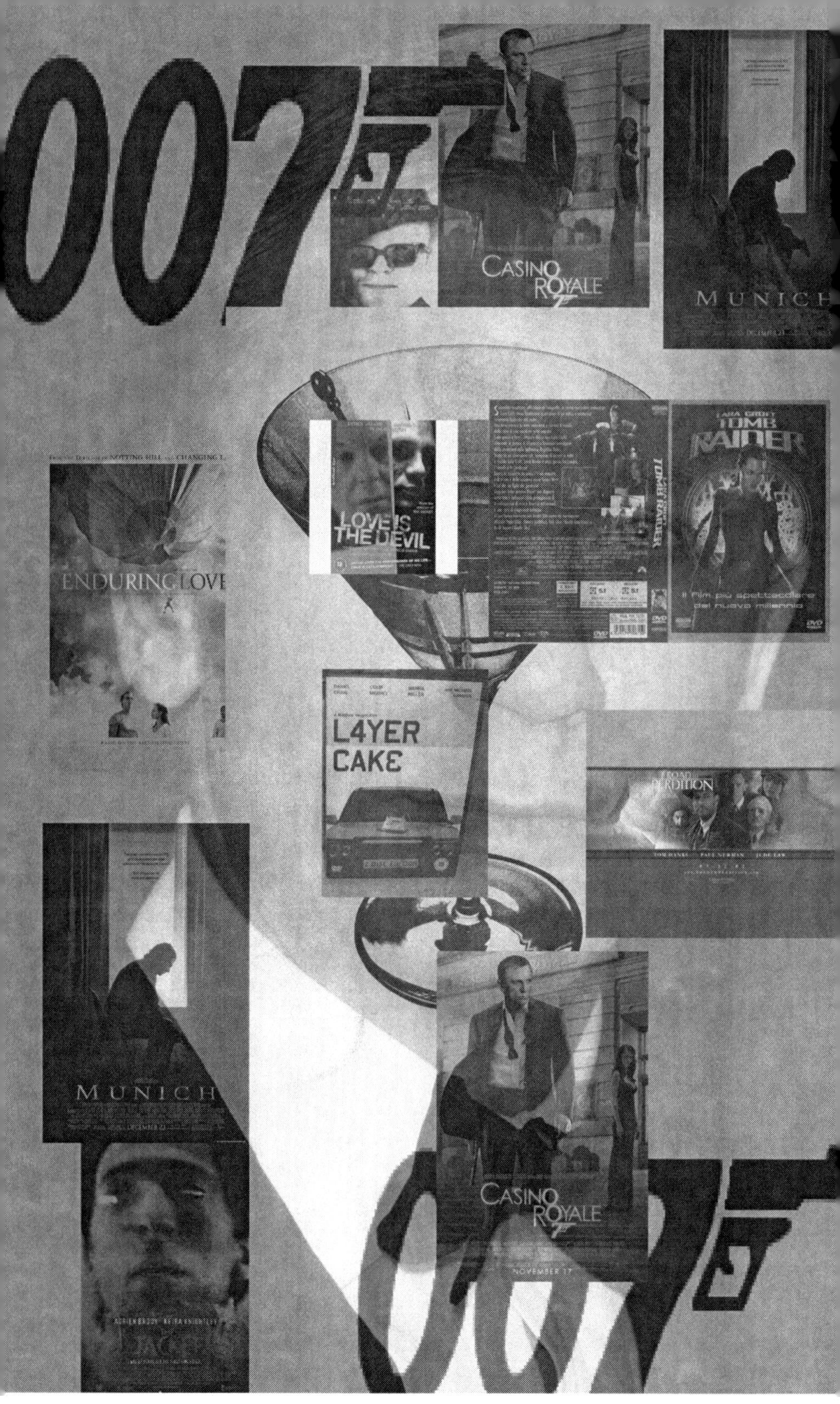

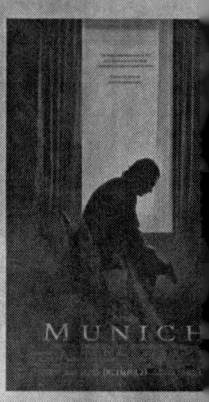

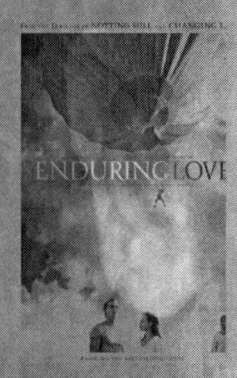

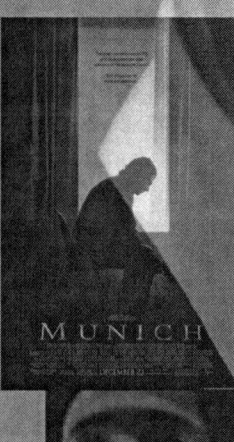

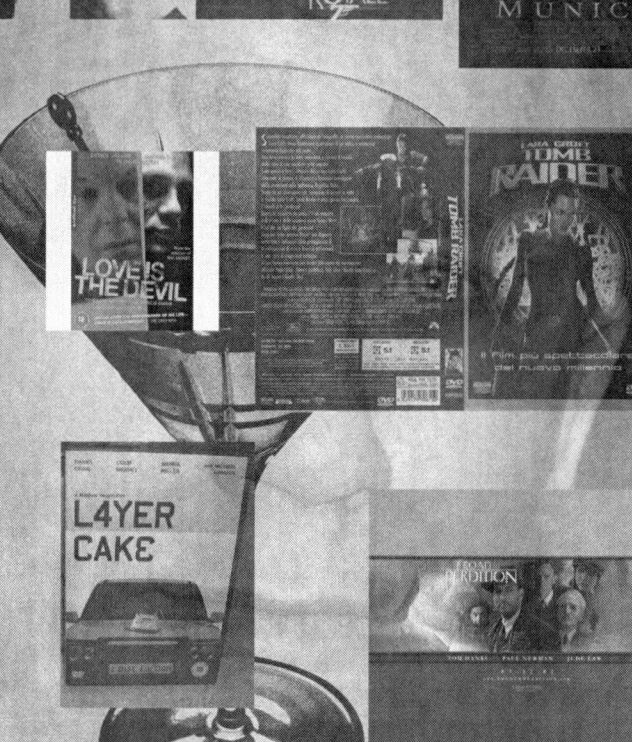

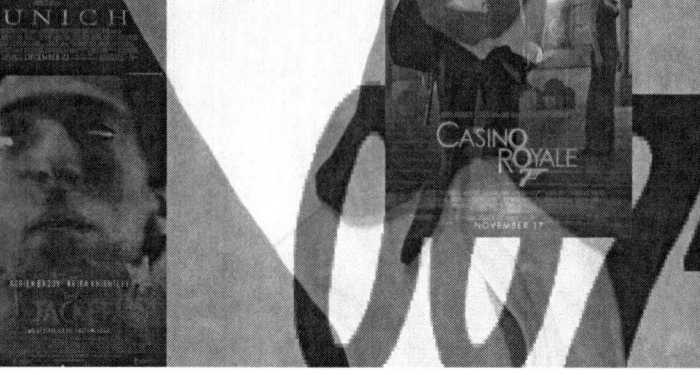

CONTENTS

Introduction — 7

Ch 1 Our Friends in the North — 13

Ch 2 Craig Steps into the Limelight... Reluctantly — 47

Ch 3 Redemption from the Limelight in Perdition — 73

Ch 4 James Bond or James Bland? — 127

Conclusion — 155

I go through life thinking it's all going to end tomorrow.

Daniel Craig

INTRODUCTION

Thanks to his starring role as the new James Bond in *Casino Royale*, Daniel Craig is now one of the most famous actors in the world. Previously known chiefly for his ability to get under the skin of some complex, unusual and often controversial characters, he suddenly became an overnight sensation and a household name after silencing his critics with what many argued was the best performance ever given by a Bond actor.

Few can fault Daniel's talents, but his success is surprising for two reasons. Firstly, he has usually preferred to focus on far less high-profile projects. He first came to the public's awareness as would-be porn baron Geordie Peacock in the BBC's 1996 drama *Our Friends in the North*. Immediately before then he had been scratching a living doing whatever he could – theatre, small TV parts, even waiting tables. He was absolutely broke and, emotionally, at the lowest he had ever been, with a failed marriage and three years of apparently fruitless acting training at the Guildhall behind him. Occasionally, he has said, he even had to sleep on park benches because he couldn't afford to pay his rent.

Nonetheless, he kept to his chosen craft and gradually he began to make his mark. And when the opportunities finally started to come his way, he stayed true to that craft. He didn't go for the highest paid films with the best publicity. Instead, he looked for less commercial, independent projects but ones that despite appealing to smaller audiences would challenge him as an actor. It was only later that – with some misgivings – he started to work on larger, more lucrative projects. Even then, he would still alternate these with theatre appearances and art house films.

Secondly, Daniel is that rarest of breeds: a famous actor who eschews the limelight. Virtually alone in an industry that thrives on press interest, he prefers a low-key lifestyle and does everything he can to avoid paparazzi and the media. And he means it. This is not a pose designed to attract, as it is with some actors who make the same claim, the very attention that it seeks to disavow.

'I don't believe in self-promotion,' he has said. 'Really, I can't be arsed.' In fact, he was so dismayed by the publicity at the beginning of his career that he stopped doing lifestyle interviews altogether. It has now been over ten years since he spoke more than a few words about anything personal to the press. In the early days, he barely even talked about his work, although he now realises that he can hardly avoid this. He noted:

Self-promotion, for me, is like going to the dentist. But I know I have to do it. It is much easier than it was. I can bullshit better these days.

Everything about the actor is understated. Instead of the tailored clothes that his co-stars favour, he prefers to buy his corduroy trousers from Marks & Spencer's. In the evenings, he favours a quiet pub with a few pints of Guinness rather than a night on the dancefloor of an exclusive club (or even a night in with a PlayStation). Even his looks do not have typical movie-star qualities. Unlike the primped, metrosexual appearances so common in the film world, his face – which earned him the childhood nickname of 'Mr Potato Head' – has a more rugged appeal.

'I just don't pursue *celebrity*, for want of a better word,' he says. 'I've got nothing against it, it's just not for me. You know, I've got other things to do and, if I'm not working, I don't want to be sitting around talking about myself.' He does his best to lead an intensely private life, although in the past couple of years his brief relationships with Kate Moss and Sienna Miller have introduced him to the circus of media interest that surrounds many of his contemporaries. The role of James Bond has pushed him further than ever into the public eye, but he still intends to preserve that anonymity, keeping his work and personal life separate.

'I don't want Daniel Craig to be known about,' he says simply. 'That has got nothing to do with anybody.' Daniel himself is fully aware of the problems that this kind of approach has for a famous actor. He is now followed by paparazzi wherever he goes and has to deal with journalists digging around for whatever they can get. 'If someone in my past decides they want to write about me, there's nothing I can do about it,' he told *The Guardian*. 'It's their thing, it's what they're paid to do. But if it's to do with my present group of friends, my family, then there is a need for some control to be taken because that's private.'

INTRODUCTION

In the past, this unusual desire for privacy has been mistaken for prickliness or, worse still, dullness. Some have mistaken his disinclination for self-promotion as aloofness. In reality, he just knows where his priorities lie. 'You do meet actors who have no life,' Nick Reding, one of his closest friends, told *The Independent,* 'but Daniel has a huge life, and many friends, and a fabulous girlfriend: he's extraordinarily well-rounded.'

For all the drawbacks, Daniel is stunned by how quickly his career took off and his new status as a global star. 'I go through life thinking it's all going to end tomorrow,' he once said, though there is little danger of that any more. With eleven years of critically-acclaimed work behind him and a promising future ahead, it is clear that Daniel Craig's career is far from over.

CH 1

OUR FRIENDS IN THE NORTH

Daniel Wroughton Craig was born at home on March 2, 1968. There was nothing remotely out of the ordinary about his beginnings. His parents lived at 41 Liverpool Road, Chester, in an 1869 Victorian town house – now a Bed and Breakfast – not far from the city centre. Legend (as recorded by *The Sun*, anyway) has it that the midwife wrapped the new baby in a copy of *The Guardian* before handing him to his parents; hardly auspicious beginnings for a world-famous actor. His mother, 'Carol' Olivia Craig, was an art teacher. His father, Tim, used to be a merchant seaman who later in life turned to a job in construction, as a steel erector, before settling on a more sedate career as the landlord of the Ring O' Bells pub in Frodsham, Cheshire, and finally working as a recruitment boss. Daniel was the their second child – he was preceded by his sister Lea.

Four years after he was born, his parents split up. The

young Daniel went to live with his mother and sister. Despite his hard-man image, he insists that there was nothing especially tough about his childhood, although on one rare occasion when he did choose to answer a question about the effect his upbringing had on him, he hinted that the situation with his parents had been less than perfect. 'I had a fantastic youth. Both of my parents are still alive, thank goodness, and they supported me in their own way,' he said – hardly a ringing endorsement, though he was quick to qualify it. 'I could make up stories for you and some of them are true, but I don't consider my life tough in any way.'

There is no question that it was Olivia who sparked his passion for acting. His mum had attended Liverpool Art College, where John Lennon had studied – despite failing his 'O' Levels – and founded the Beatles. She managed to gain a place at RADA, the Royal Academy of Dramatic Art in London. Even though this was one of the most highly-regarded drama schools in the world, she declined her place, instead going into motherhood and teaching. In this respect, Daniel was lucky; many parents fail to understand their children's thespian leanings and actively encourage them against a career in acting. In Olivia's case, it was exactly the opposite.

After his parents divorced, Olivia took Daniel and Lea and moved to central Liverpool, where she had lived as a girl. It was only a few miles away and Daniel would get to see his dad on a regular basis. Although his parents had split up, the divorce was less disruptive in terms of his schooling; he could still attend Frodsham Church of England Primary School, in the same village where his dad ran the Ring O' Bells. They would later move again to Hoylake, Wirral, Olivia's childhood home.

Daniel Craig at Hoylake Church of England Primary School, Wirrall, England.

Daniel's interest in the stage started when his mother began to take him on visits to the Everyman Theatre in Liverpool. Located on Hope Street (also home to the Liverpool College of Art), the Everyman had been founded in the mid-60s with the aim of showing plays that had particular relevance to Liverpudlian life. Despite this apparently niche appeal, the theatre has been the launching platform for the careers of such greats as Bill Nighy and Julie Walters.

Although he didn't tread the boards himself, the theatre had a formative influence on Daniel, too. 'It was the Everyman which got me into acting. Liverpool Art College and Manchester Polytechnic were producing all these great things and my mum helped with the stage design and it was part of her social life, it was where she hung out. I'd see the plays or I would be in the lighting box backstage and I knew that was what I wanted to do,' he said. Clearly impressed by the characters he met in the theatre, he decided to become the same himself. 'I guess I just wanted to show off,' he told *Interview* magazine. 'A lot of my mother's contemporaries were actors – they were larger than life.' His resolve barely faltered in the following years, even when he later discovered the reason for their charisma. 'I found out they were just pissed. Drunk,' he said.

Daniel's own stage debut took place at the age of six, in a primary school production of *Oliver!* Soon after this he surprised his father with his intentions. 'I remember having some friends over and Daniel was just weaving in and out between their legs,' Tim Craig said in an interview with *Contact Music*. 'One asked him what he was going to do when he grew up and without breaking stride he said, "Be an actor." I remember at the time blinking and doing a double take, because he said it with such certainty and he was so small.'

After 30 years, school headmaster Peter Mason still remembers Daniel, too. 'Even at the ages of five and six it isn't very difficult to tell when someone has real ability and talent. We encouraged pupils to take part in prayers and to perform little plays in front of the parents. Both Daniel and his older sister Lia were very good. I could tell even then that Daniel was gifted – I was sorry when they left the school.'

In 1973, Tim took his five-year-old son to see his first Bond film. Daniel has always maintained that Roger Moore's *Live and Let Die* has held a special place in his heart ever since as a result. He was in the minority amongst his contemporaries, who were never allowed to watch the films. 'Bond was something we knew about but never got to see,' said Anthony Lewis, a contemporary of Daniel's, whose aunt married Tim around the same time. We wanted to watch but we were too young.' His early memories of the now rugged and muscled actor, now a heartthrob to millions of women (and not a few men) the world over, are not complimentary. 'He was always gangly, with a pudding bowl haircut, not what you'd call cool. His hair was so blond it was almost white,' he recalled of his friend. 'Daniel was a lot of fun to be with. We'd play football or go to the zoo and he would come and sleep over. Sometimes we had to share a bed so now I can say I've slept with James Bond! I remember us all going to the movies together – but back then I never imagined that one day Daniel would be up there on screen.'

Critics of his own recent anointing as the sixth Bond were disappointed to learn that *Live and Let Die* was both the first and the last of the films that he took the trouble to watch in the cinema. 'I think that was in

1973,' he said. 'The last time I paid to see a Bond film would be 1973! Except no, my dad paid!' Despite his apparent ambivalence to the franchise, he still credits the spy with bringing him back to the idea of an acting career after briefly toying with alternatives. 'At ten, I wanted to be a marine biologist but that was probably because I'd seen *Jaws*.' Film, it seems, was a persuasive medium for the young Daniel. 'I always came back to acting though. I think I was initially influenced by movies like James Bond – and the thought of dressing up and showing off. But when I got older, I came to believe acting was kind of a worthwhile thing to do.'

'He was always performing, I would catch him tap dancing in school outside the offices,' Olivia remembers of her son. Daniel says she still has an essay he wrote when he was six years old, claiming he wanted to be an actor. Between the trips to the theatre with his mother and the ones to the cinema with his father and school friends, there was never any real doubt in his mind. 'I got the bug and it was as simple as that,' he said in an interview with *eFilmCritic*. 'Things have changed as I have gotten older but the same things still apply – dressing up, showing off and the attention-seeking are still there. I love it. I think it is a great art form – it is a populist art form that I do believe can actually change things and generate discussion and debate. I remember that we had a cinema around the corner from me and I would sit there and watch movies.

'One particular movie was *Blade Runner* and even though I had no idea what was happening, I watched it and I knew that I wanted to make movies. It wasn't about doing films or television or plays – I wanted to do movies and that one struck me the first time that I saw it.'

As a young child, Daniel would spend some of his holidays with his mother's parents, Olwyn and Doris Williams. On one occasion when he was eight, they took him on a cruise of the Norwegian fjords. Daniel surprised the other passengers and crew by writing and acting his own show for them.

When he was nine, the family moved again, this time to Hoylake on the west coast of the Wirrel. Soon after, like her ex-husband, Olivia also found someone new – artist and musician Max Blond. Adam Brierley was one of the first friends Daniel made in his new home. 'Danny and I had been friends since we were nine,' Adam later told the Liverpool Echo. 'He moved in a couple of roads away from my parents' house so I invited him to play football with us on the beach. After that we were friends through most of our school life.'

The pair attended Hilbre High School in West Kirby. Daniel never got much out of his formal education. Despite coming across as perfectly intelligent and articulate today, in both his films and in interviews, he failed his 11+. The problem was not ability but motivation: he just didn't see the point. The only real draw of school was the opportunity for acting. 'I didn't like school that much, but I got into drama and that was really the key for me, I found my impetus then,' he said. As a teacher, his mum wanted more for him, knowing that ability is important but that qualifications go a long way too. 'She wanted me to get a real education, but that failed miserably,' he joked.

He has only mentioned a few events from these years. Since his leap to worldwide fame, he has become more reluctant than ever to give the public a window into his childhood and personal life. One is an early, never-to-be-repeated attempt at shoplifting.

'Me and my mates were standing in a corner shop and they suddenly grabbed a pack of crisps and ran. Nobody told me that was the plan so I was a bit slow.' The shopkeeper was quicker off the mark and stopped him before he even got out of the door. 'I grabbed a pack but was nabbed straight away,' he said. 'I was like, "What? I was going to pay for it." I had to take the rap for everybody. I was a crap thief. I never did it again.'

In fact, what he and his friends have told about his childhood is quite at odds with his current image. The skinny, spotty boy was a fan of poetry and remembers being particularly impacted by the gift of a book – Ted Hughes' *Crow* – on his tenth birthday. On one occasion, he even decided to sneak into the local girls' grammar school to hear the poet himself reading from his work. He remembers being disappointed by Hughes' monotonous recital.

Boy Band

It wasn't just acting that interested Daniel. He was

keen on any opportunity to take the limelight. Adam Brierley remembers their decision to form a rock group. 'In secondary school my friend Paul Donnelly and I decided to put together a band,' he told the *Liverpool Echo*. 'We wanted a charismatic frontman, but our voices were breaking – not exactly rock star material. I thought Danny would be perfect. He was very confident. He had a real presence on stage, he was always in stage shows – you could see how good he was even then. Danny was always saying he wanted to be an actor and he was very good. I remember seeing him in the school plays and you could see his potential. His step-dad was an artist and in a jazz band and I was always in bands from the age of seven, so I liked going round to his house to see the instruments and equipment.'

Another classmate, Chris, remembers how this was a source of tension. 'Danny and I were friends at school until he replaced me in the school rock band,' he recalled. 'All because he, or rather his dad I think, had a microphone and I didn't. I was gutted and never spoke to him again!'

Appearances are clearly deceptive; photos and his contemporaries' recollections describe a gangling, geeky kid. Despite this, he was confident and charismatic – and loved to show it on stage – but wasn't arrogant about his abilities. 'Daniel wasn't full of himself at all,' remembers Rob Fennah, who worked with them in the band. 'He was very quiet – the spotty one at the back with a big flick haircut.

He was always a nice lad.' Daniel's slightly unusual head shape and jug ears earned him the nickname 'Mr Potato Head' among his classmates – one that has stuck ever since.

His music teacher, Mrs Milne, remembers his talent on the guitar, although it was his acting skills that really drew her attention. Like the others, she remembers him as a quiet pupil who didn't go out of his way to get himself noticed, saving his talent for the stage. 'He was a nice, affable boy who never sought any glory,' she said. 'He had a good voice and a definite presence. We knew he was special – a good face, good bone structure and he could play lots of parts.'

The three friends pulled in another couple of class-mates from their school year, Paul King and Andy Fennah, on rhythm and lead guitar, and they were set to go. 'We'd been mates for years,' remembered Andy. 'We were all into music so it seemed the natural thing to be in a band together.' The consensus among staff and pupils was that they were actually pretty impressive. 'We used to do gigs at school and we entered a few competitions.'

Daniel came up with the name for the band, the Inner Voices. This was actually a reference to a little-known play about Imperial Russia that he had seen at the Everyman and been particularly struck by. 'The name for the band was Danny's idea,' remembers Adam. 'He was very into the theatre. We all liked the name and it stuck.'

1: OUR FRIENDS IN THE NORTH

Adam remembers one occasion, when they were 16, when Inner Voices played in front of the school. 'In our final year the headmaster, Wally Bruce, was having a leaving concert,' he recalled. 'He was very religious and it was billed as a highbrow event with classical music, but we somehow managed to get a slot for Inner Voices. Trying to be rebellious we played a rocked up version of "The House Of The Rising Sun".'

Instead of the shocked reaction they were all hoping for, the five were stunned when the ballad – which is about a brothel – was met with thunderous applause. 'To our horror we found out The Animals were Mr Bruce's favourite band!' They were considered so good that Andy's brothers, Rob (who is now a professional musician) and Alan took them to a studio to record their version of the song.

'I took them into the recording studio with their teacher,' said Rob laconically. 'They weren't bad actually. It was all done live – we didn't have time to lay down different tracks, so it wandered a bit, but the end result was OK.'

Apart from the stage, Daniel's other passion was for rugby. Once he grew out of his skinny adolescent body he turned out to be a decent player. He was on the school team and also played for Hoylake RUFC. His father claims that, had he not gone into acting, he probably would have continued his career on the rugby pitch. He was also a keen football fan, supporting Liverpool FC – though there were limits to his loyalty.

His Dark Materials - The Golden Compass, 2007

He remembers being offered, and having to turn down, a ticket to watch his team play Chelsea. 'A friend of mine got seats at Chelsea and I said, "I'm not going to fucking sit at the Chelsea end to watch Liverpool play! If Liverpool scored a goal, I would have to jump in the air. Then I would get killed!"'

Young Talent

It was always clear to his contemporaries where he was destined to end up. His drama teachers and others were quick to heap praise on the young Daniel, whose abilities, even as a young teenager, were so clear to them. Brenda Davies, who taught at Hilbre, remembers him trying out for a role in a school production (*Oliver!* again) in 1981. 'My jaw nearly hit the floor when he got up on stage,' she later said. 'He had such timing and range and he had stage presence for a 13-year-old. I thought "What have we here?"'

She wasn't the only one to be impressed. Hilary Green, his drama teacher, also saw his audition. She says that Daniel had come in with a friend and, initially at least, had not wanted to try for a part. 'From the very first we knew we had something special,' she remembers. 'His good looks, voice, personality, and an indefinable something, combined to make him riveting on stage. He was quite exceptional.'

He secured the part of Mr Sowerberry, the Undertaker, and stole the show. Having proved himself this early on, things would only get better. 'Daniel was a natural on the stage, and he showed it in his first role in

Oliver!,' said Hilary. 'From then on I made sure we gave him every opportunity to develop. We worked together closely for three years, and he tried quite a few different things. He was always remarkably mature for his years, and he had a real edge.'

After his success in *Oliver!* he was given the lead part in the school's next production – Arthur Miller's tale of the 1692 Salem Witch Trials and allegory of 1950s American politics, *The Crucible*. Following that, he took the lead in *Romeo and Juliet*. On both occasions, audiences were left impressed. 'He excelled as Proctor in *The Crucible*, a highly serious role, but he could also be quite funny,' recounted Hilary. 'As one of the Ugly Sisters in Cinderella, he reduced the audience and cast to helpless laughter. It brought the production to a standstill for a while. It was his natural sense of inflection and timing that made his performance so effective. The pair of them were absolutely hilarious and had the audience in stitches every night.'

Daniel's co-star, Richard Kelly, remembers the fun they had dressing up in drag and working the audience's sense of humour. 'It was a real scream,' he said. 'Daniel was great in the show, playing it for laughs. One night he took a water pistol and trained it on the orchestra.' It wasn't the first time that Daniel had played this role. 'He also was an Ugly Sister at the age of eight at his primary school,' his mother claimed. (Even from that early age, it seems that Daniel was willing to push the boundaries – a tendency more fully and shockingly explored in some of his more recent films.)

Today, Daniel displays an incredible range of talent. Unlike many actors, he has never been typecast into a particular role or genre, as can so easily happen. In his films, he has played a bewildering array of characters, always reluctant to cover the same ground twice. This keen desire (and ability) for self-development was something he showed at school and that stood him in good stead in the following years when he would need to audition for every part going. 'He had an innate ability to step into the skin of a character, and was extremely versatile,' said Hilary. 'It was a sign of his acting talent that he was prepared to have a go at anything. He was good as Moon in Tom Stoppard's *The Real Inspector Hound*, and I made sure he got a part in the Bleasdale play being put on by the Woolgatherers.'

This was a reference to a play by Alan Bleasdale, *No More Sitting On The Old School Bench*, which was put on by a local amateur dramatic society, the Heswall Woolgatherers. He featured in the play along with his girlfriend, Helen Gowland. Helen, who was with Daniel for two years, remembers him fondly. 'He was a lovely lad and I'm sure he hasn't changed much,' she told the *Liverpool Echo*. 'He still looks much like he did when he was 15. We were close and I have really good memories of Daniel.' The pair parted ways when Daniel went to London to study acting and Helen took a job as a secretary. But there were no hard feelings. 'I am really pleased he has gone on to make such a success of himself,' she said.

Trudy Kilpatrick, another of his contemporaries at Hilbre, remembers of the teenager, 'He had ambition and you knew he was going to go on and do something. People looked up to him because he was a good actor and a few girls fancied him because he was so talented.'

Daniel Dweeb?

Most of his classmates' and teachers' memories of Daniel are complimentary. The picture they give is of a quiet student who, despite an obvious talent for acting and love of the stage, didn't boast about his abilities and never assumed he was above his friends and contemporaries. Perhaps he wasn't the best-looking kid in the class, but a few spots are nothing unusual for 16-year-olds and jug-ears aren't the end of the world. In characteristically iconoclastic style, though, the *Mail on Sunday* dug around after he was named as the new Bond in 2005, and managed to find themselves a dissenting voice.

Ann Hudson-Gardner was another schoolmate, though a year or two older than Daniel. Like him, she was involved in the school production of Stoppard's *The Real Inspector Hound*, a parody of the typical parlour mystery, in which three theatre critics gather to review a play. Ann's memories of him are less forgiving than those of his friends and teachers. 'He wasn't a babe-magnet by any stretch of the imagination,' she remembered fondly. 'Bless him, he did have trouble with acne and he was seen by most people as a bit of a dweeb.'

Even she had to relent, though, after watching him in his recent roles. 'Seeing him now, those battles with spots have left him with craggy good looks. But then he didn't leave the girls feeling shaken or stirred. He was a bit full of himself.' The boy she describes is an aloof loner, someone totally different from the person his friends remember. 'Danny always said he was going to be an actor – stressing the last syllable – but he never boasted he wanted to be James Bond. He was very serious, there was no joviality about him.'

'He didn't have a life,' she continued accusingly. 'There were a few parties and he was invited, but he didn't go.' She recalls an occasion when the cast needed his help on their return from staging their play. 'On the way back from Liverpool the minibus broke down. We got off to push – but he didn't, he was far too grand.'

Suffice to say that few other sources share her unfavourable impressions of the teenaged Daniel. In the wake of his recent fame, his father was certainly quick to hit back at rumours that his son was a sissy after being knocked about whilst filming a fight scene. 'At 15, Daniel was playing rugby for Birkenhead Park Colts. He can look after himself all right. As a lad he was a tough rugby player and he would probably have become a professional if things hadn't turned out differently. He used to work behind the bar of a pub in Portobello Road, London, and he could certainly handle himself if fights kicked off.'

Jacqueline Stormes, mother of his school friend Tim, also

recalls him in a better light than Ann. 'Daniel and Tim had been great friends, both members of Hoylake Rugby Club. I remember his rich deep voice, very melodic and smooth.' Her daughter Samantha, now 35, remembers being impressed too. 'He had a voice as smooth as chocolate, and eyes like ice,' she said.

His three years under the tuition of Hilary Green was invaluable, and Daniel has remembered her efforts to encourage his career ever since. When he was establishing himself on the London stage some years later, he thought enough of her to send her a signed programme from one of his performances, with the note 'Thanks for setting me on the way, love Daniel.'

Pastures New

Although Daniel was never the most academically gifted student, he made enough of an effort after his failed 11-plus to get the results he needed to go to the grammar school in nearby Calday. 'He was conscientious and did well enough at GCSEs to attend the local grammar,' said his mother. However, by this time Daniel had realised that there was little point in toiling away over his A-levels when he figured he would never use them. His family already knew that acting was the only career he was interested in, and his mother remembers him telling her that 'qualifications on bits of paper weren't going to get him there.'

'After two terms he said he had realised that it wasn't for him,' Olivia recalled. 'It was his intention to ditch his studies and go to London instead to study acting.'

His mother was disturbed by the idea of leaving school before he finished his studies, and convened a family meeting. 'It must have been very hard as he knew I had my heart set on university for him,' she said. But she also knew his potential, and that this was what he really wanted, so rather than banning him from taking up his dream she made a deal with him. 'Before he dropped out I said if he wasn't going to university, he must promise to get into a top drama school – or go back to school.' She even helped him to apply to the National Youth Theatre, arranging his audition with them while the troupe were on tour in Manchester in 1984. To Daniel's surprise and delight, he was accepted. Despite the fact that he was only 16, he left his A-levels at Calday Grammar behind and moved to London to train with the NYT.

Life was a blast but it wasn't an easy time. Money was very short and he was forced to find work wherever he could get it – often waiting tables and working in restaurant kitchens at anti-social hours of the day. He has spoken about having to sleep on friends' floors (and sometimes park benches), and occasionally doing a runner from a rented property because he couldn't afford to pay the landlord. But at least the NYT provided a focus for him, and the acting opportunities they gave him made the work and hardships worthwhile. 'They were a huge influence on my life,' he said. 'They give people like me the support zone to concentrate on acting, because London's such a bastard of a place to live in if you're 16 or 17. Actually, it can be awful at any time of life if you don't have any money.'

1: OUR FRIENDS IN THE NORTH

His first appearance on the stage with NYT was in Shakespeare's *Troilus and Cressida*, as Agamemnon. His parents came down to London to watch him on the first night. Under director Edward Wilson, he would tour with the troupe to Spain and Russia.

The next step in his plan was to get into drama school, but it wasn't as easy as he had hoped. Daniel applied to a range of different places but was repeatedly turned down. It took more than two years and repeated applications before he was successful. All the while, he was scratching work wherever he could find it, 'doing every job known to man.'

He was 19 before – on his third audition – he was finally accepted into the Guildhall School of Music and Drama at the Barbican, in 1988. It was a three year-long course under Colin McCormack of the Royal Shakespeare Company. He was amongst some talented peers, overlapping in his time there with Ewan McGregor, Alistair McGowan, Damian Lewis and Joseph Fiennes.

He graduated in 1991 after 'three years at Guildhall, where they teach you how you're not going to be employed,' as he has jokingly referred to his time there. He appreciated the formal training, but understood that one of the biggest lessons he learnt was about motivation. 'I got a lot out of it, but mainly I realized I had to get out of bed in the morning and take it seriously,' he told *Cinema Confidential*.

Sylvia, 2004

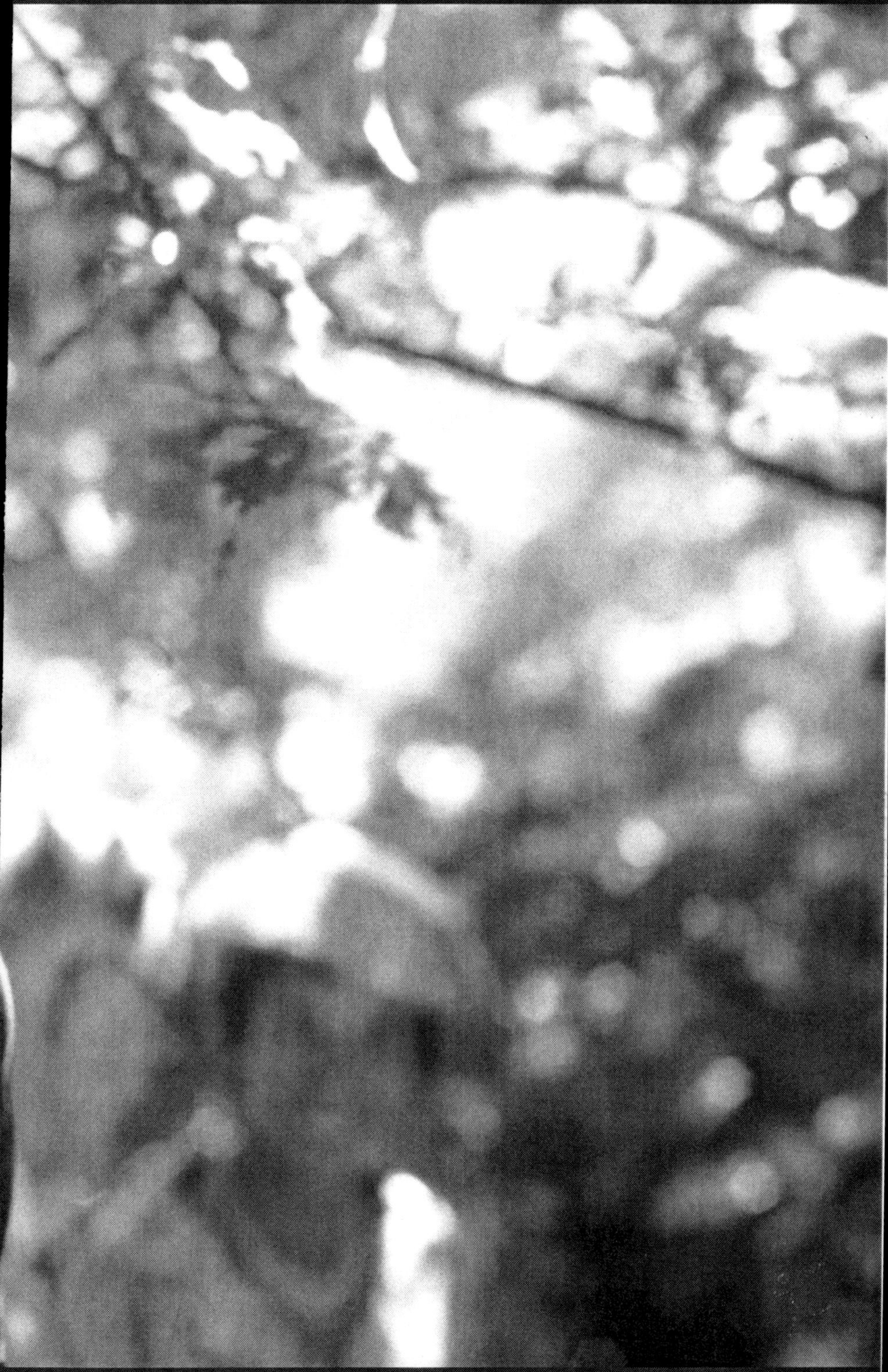

Infamous

There are always a few embarrassing skeletons locked in the closet from anyone's university days, and Daniel Craig is no exception. And the brighter the limelight, the more willing journalists are to shine it into those dark corners of celebrities' lives that they hoped everyone else had forgotten about. In this case, the tabloid to search out the slowly rotting corpses of indiscretions past was the *Daily Mail* – an interesting coincidence, given that their sister paper the *Mail on Sunday* had run the 'Daniel Dweeb' story almost exactly a year earlier in November 2005.

'Tearing a letter open with idle curiosity,' ran the article, 'the pretty young woman's eyes widened in shock. Staring back at her was the face of a fellow student with whom she had shared a drunken one-night stand. It wasn't his face that had startled her, however, despite the would-be seductive look in his eye. The photograph – one of several she received – was singularly revealing.'

The unnamed woman, according to the *Daily Mail* in its continuing crusade against the actor, promptly burned the photo and the others that followed (thereby denying herself a small fortune in later years from the opportunity of selling them to an agency like Big Pictures). Rather than being the toned, confident, athletic man of his later years, the subject is described as 'a bit of a geek', with 'lank, greasy hair, spotty face, introspective and somewhat awkward manner.'

The *Daily Mail's* so-called source suggested that the

two had, in fact, got together for a one-night stand, but that Daniel had seen it as the start of something more significant and long-term. 'The girl was mortified,' recalls a friend. 'She had slept with him when she was drunk one night – she suspected she may have taken his virginity – and he became really keen on her.'

Twenty years ago at the Guildhall, the friend suggested, Daniel was not the heartthrob he is now. 'She was quite a fashionable girl and very much part of the in-crowd, while Daniel was just a hanger-on really. They all thought of him as vaguely diverting but hopelessly uncool.' (If this is true, the boot is on the other foot these days; Daniel spends his time amongst one of the most talked-about cliques of the day, the illustrious Primrose Hill Set, a group of fast-living high-fliers who at that time had colonised the district just to the north of London's Regent's Park).

'She had wanted to forget all about it,' the source continued, 'but soon found out that what was just a drunken one-off to her was seen by Daniel as something a lot more serious. He thought it was the beginning of a beautiful and lasting romance, whereas she just thought, "Oh gosh, how embarrassing!" He was so desperate to win her over that he started sending her revealing photographs of himself. But all he succeeded in doing was making himself look even more ridiculous. Needless to say, they didn't end up going out together.' Romantically linked to the likes of Kate Moss and Sienna Miller in the past few years, things have changed an awful lot for Daniel.

'To the people who knew him back then it is beyond incredible that he is the new James Bond,' the friend continued. 'As far as they're concerned it isn't the slightest bit surprising that some people have been critical about the casting.'

Others from his class were equally ready to put the boot in on the *Daily Mail's* behalf when they learned of his new film role. 'It's quite interesting that some people said he was too ugly to be Bond,' one was quoted, 'because this is somebody who all his life has never quite fitted in. You had to feel sorry for Daniel because he was a talented actor who has worked incredibly hard for his success. But when he finally hit the big time as Bond he found himself back at square one: everyone was criticising him for being ugly and uncool. It must have been horrible for him.'

Enduring Love?

One person who clearly didn't find him repellent was Fiona Loudon (now better known as Harley), a Scottish stage actress and singer who began dating him towards the end of his time at Guildhall. Daniel must have been doing something right because Harley was five months pregnant when the two decided to get married in July, 1992. The ceremony took place in Edinburgh, where she was originally from, although the rest of the time they shared a flat together in Fulham, London. Their daughter Ella was born towards the end of that year.

If Daniel is cagey about his own personal life, he is even more so about those of his daughter and ex-wife. Ella, who is now 15, is said to be a gifted actress herself. 'I don't bring her up in conversations much because the more I talk about her the more the Press have a right to take those photographs,' Daniel once said.

His relationship with the blonde jazz singer did not last long and in 1994 they divorced. Although he remains characteristically laconic about the failed marriage, he has made the occasional comment about it in the past. Back in 1996, before he had learned to stay silent and totally given up doing lifestyle interviews altogether, he admitted his misgivings about the way things worked out. 'I was 23 when I got married, I was too young,' he told *The Independent*. 'I don't know if it was a mistake exactly, but it was not the right thing to do at the time. I don't regret it, but I do wish I'd lived it in a different way.'

Two-year-old Ella stayed with her mother after the divorce. After the failure of both his parents' marriage and his own, he could be forgiven for having doubts about tying the knot again. But Daniel maintains that he simply didn't grasp what it meant to be married. 'I do believe in marriage. I really do,' he told *The Telegraph*. 'I believe that getting together with somebody and making a public statement about it is a good thing. I just didn't really understand it before. Commitment is part of a life. The toughest part, probably.'

After leaving drama school, success didn't just drop into his lap. 'I was a jobbing actor, just doing what I could,' he says. There were occasional parts in films and TV programmes, and he spent a year at the National Theatre. 'I was out of work for seven or eight months, but I wasn't penniless and starving. I had an overdraft. This is the modern world, I just owed the bank a lot of money.' Work came in dribs and drabs, and there was a certain similarity between many of his early roles. 'When I first started, villains were all I did. I'm blond and blue-eyed, so they always gave me the part of the Nazi. When I started getting roles that were goodies, I didn't really know what to do with them, I just wanted to thump people.'

Daniel has complained in the past that the only roles open to him when he began acting for a living were 'Nazis and fops'. He has certainly played a few of both in his 15-year-long career. His training at the Guildhall – as well as his early experiences at the Everyman in Liverpool – left him with a dislike for costume drama and the more pretentious roles. 'I don't want to be dressing up in costumes and pansying around,' he said. 'When I left drama school the only jobs were for boys with floppy fringes who went to Eton. I could fit in because I could do a slightly posh accent. But I realised actually I can't really be posh.'

To begin with, the future looked bright. Almost as soon as he graduated from the Guildhall, he landed a part in a film – more than most of his classmates could hope for. Acting is a tough business in terms of finding a continuous flow of paid work. 'There is always that pessimistic optimism in actors, because you deal with so much refusal,' he said. 'But as soon as I left drama school, I went and did a Warner Brothers movie, *The Power of One*. It was the first job I ever did.'

Few budding actors are so lucky to go straight from their training into work. But it was also a baptism-by-fire into the workings of the film industry – a completely different world to the one he had been used to on his course and on theatre stages. 'It threw me into a bit of spin. It was an experience. Suddenly, I was on a shoot in Zimbabwe, on huge sets.'

The Power of One was a film about racial conflict in South Africa, told through the eyes of an English boy, P.K., sent to an Afrikaans school. Daniel played the grown up version of Jaapie Botha, a school bully with neo-Nazi tendencies who torments the orphaned protagonist until he is expelled for going too far. Years later, P.K. again crosses paths with Botha, now a sergeant in the state security force.

The film was a great start to his career, but it would be another four years before Daniel achieved any real degree of fame. At the time, he was simply an unknown and didn't stand out enough to get noticed. Still, it was a taste of what life could be like.

'It didn't work out in the sense of propelling me forward – thankfully – because it wasn't the right time or place. But I always had blind faith. I swore to myself I'd never go back to being a waiter. It was arrogance that made me stick at it.'

A handful of fairly minor roles in TV and film occurred over the next couple of years, as well as more theatre. He played the part of Schiller, a German officer in the First World War, in the *Young Indiana Jones* movie. There were forgettable parts in *Boon* and *Heartbeat*. On the stage, he starred in the Midnight Theatre Company's *No Remission* at the Lyric Theatre, Hammersmith. This play was a tense drama set in a prison cell shared by a murderer, bank robber and a violent paratrooper (played by Daniel). As chaos reigns outside, the three men gradually break down, confiding their secrets to each other. A reviewer for *The Independent* noted Daniel's cool, controlled exterior – later seen to great effect in films such as *Layer Cake* – writing that he contained his aggression 'like an unexploded mine'.

A handful of other notable roles punctuated the long periods of unemployment, when Daniel and his wife and daughter had to rely mostly on the bank-manager's goodwill to get by. There was a brief appearance in an episode of the political satire, *Drop the Dead Donkey*, then another role as a mean military type alongside Sean Bean in the 1993 *Sharpe's Eagle*. He played Lt Berry, an upper-class snob who tries to kill Sharpe, whom he regards as simply a commoner elevated to a position above himself, an 'officer from the ranks'.

Although he would play many such roles as soldiers or other kinds of hard-men in later years, he didn't go out of his way to choose them. Daniel made sure he also auditioned for other parts totally at odds with this image, such as the bitter loser in *Heartbeat* and the secretly-gay Joseph Porter Pitt in *Angels in America,* at the Royal National Theatre. In fact, *Angels* – 'a secular book of revelation to a United States that seemed to be hurtling to hell' – required him to play not one but four different roles.

By 1994 his marriage had ended and he parted company with his wife. Unlike Daniel, her career has been relatively low-key since then. She focused on theatre and music performance over movies, and her one film role was in *The Legend of Loch Lomond,* a Scottish Enterprise film. She also wrote and acted the critically-acclaimed one-woman show *Storm in a Teacup* at the Edinburgh Festival and in London. Harley is now best-known as a sultry-voiced jazz singer.

Fame

Daniel's real breakthrough into the public eye didn't happen until four years after he left drama school. For a while, it looked like he might never achieve any degree of real success. After all, he was heading for 30 and struggling to get by. Then, in 1994, he landed the role that would change his life. It was a starring part in the hit BBC drama *Our Friends in the North*.

This nine part BBC mini-series followed the lives of four friends over a 30-year period, from 1964 to 1995, from their teens to middle-age. Each episode took as its context one of these years, often set against the backdrop of a General Election to provide the political and social context for the story.

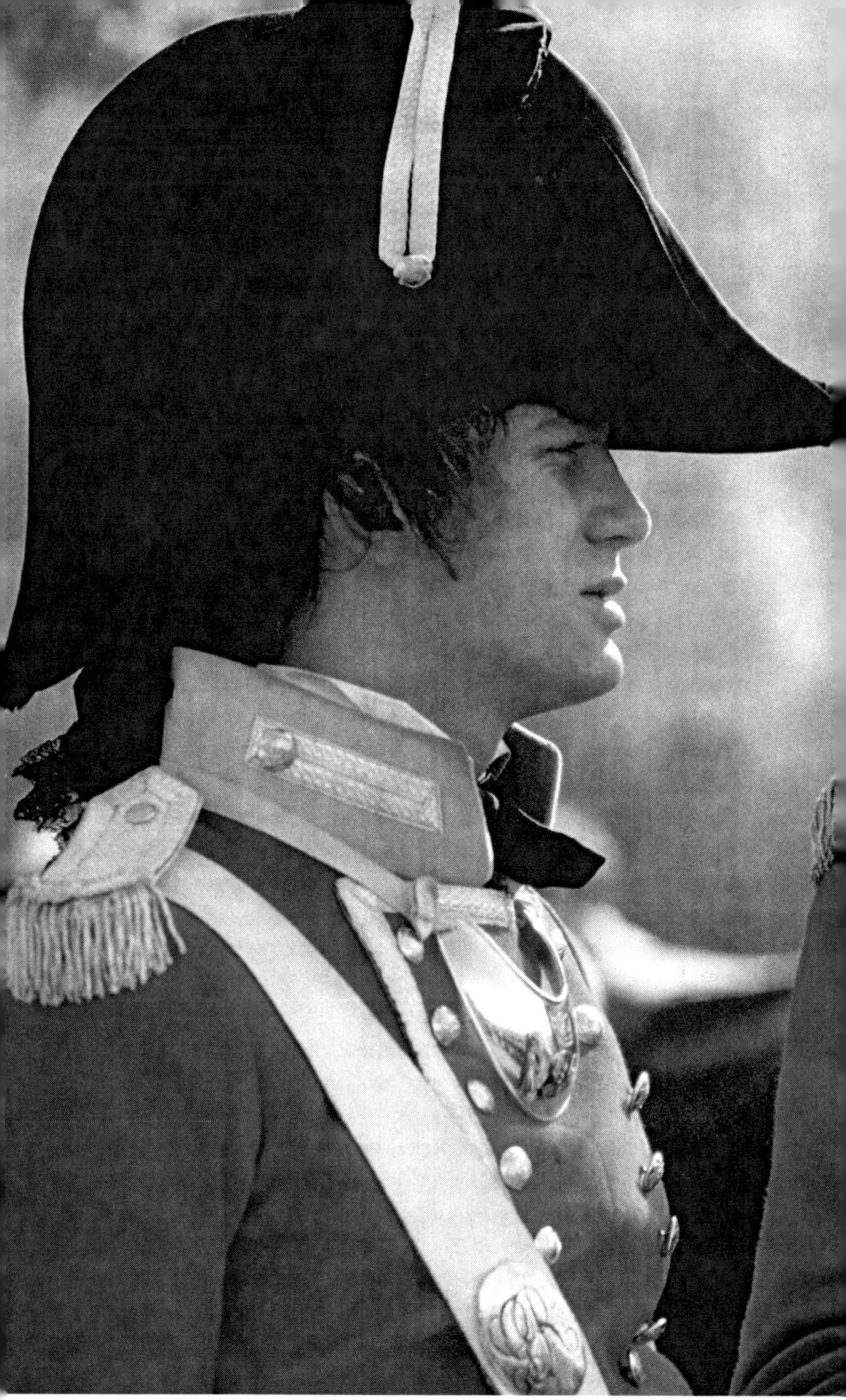

Daniel Craig and Gavan O'Herlihy: *Sharpe's Eagle,* TV series, 1993

One of the features that attracted the viewers and critics was the reconstruction of significant events and headlines from the country's past: the miner's strike of 1984, Thatcher's rise to power, political sleaze, police corruption...

Filming began in Autumn 1994 and lasted a year. It had a massive budget of £8 million – half the BBC's serial budget for that year: someone obviously had high expectations for the project. The first episode was screened in 1996 and immediately launched its cast to fame. The four actors were relative unknowns at the time of casting – all the more impressive for the careers they would progress to after this.

Christopher Eccleston, playing Nicky Hutchinson, was the best-known of the quartet, thanks to his part as DCI Dave Bilborough in ITV's *Cracker,* as well as from his role as David Stephens in1995's *Shallow Grave*. Gina McKee (who later was cast in *Notting Hill*) played Mary, Mark Strong played Tosker, and Daniel was Geordie Peacock, failed pop-star turned strip-club boss and would be porn baron. In fact, the only member of the cast with any great standing at that point was Malcolm McDowell, a name that had been box office from the early 70s when he shot to greatness in Kubrick's cult-violent *Clockwork Orange*.

CH 2

CRAIG STEPS INTO THE LIMELIGHT... RELUCTANTLY

The series was a real challenge for the four actors, playing the same characters at different ages and in different circumstances over a 30-year span. At the time, Daniel told the *Mirror* how much the previous few years had taken their toll on his self-esteem. 'Being out of work was really demoralising and I haven't ever really recovered from it,' he said. 'I was never homeless as such, but I did spend the odd night on a park bench.' He credits the series – and his co-stars and friends in the production – with drawing him out of his black moods and becoming more positive about his life. 'It helped me start to enjoy myself again,' he later told the *Independent*. 'I showed it to a friend the other day and it stood up. Gina and Mark and Chris were fantastic. They all seem fabulously real. It was because we spent time discovering things about each other. It was like being taught all over again how to make a character and get it watchable. Like a year with a Russian theatre.'

JONES BULLOCK CRAIG BOGDANOVICH DANIELS
DAVIS PALTROW ROSSELLINI STEVENSON WEAVER
INFAMOUS
There's more to the story than you know

Daniel Craig as Perry Smith: *Infamous*, 2006

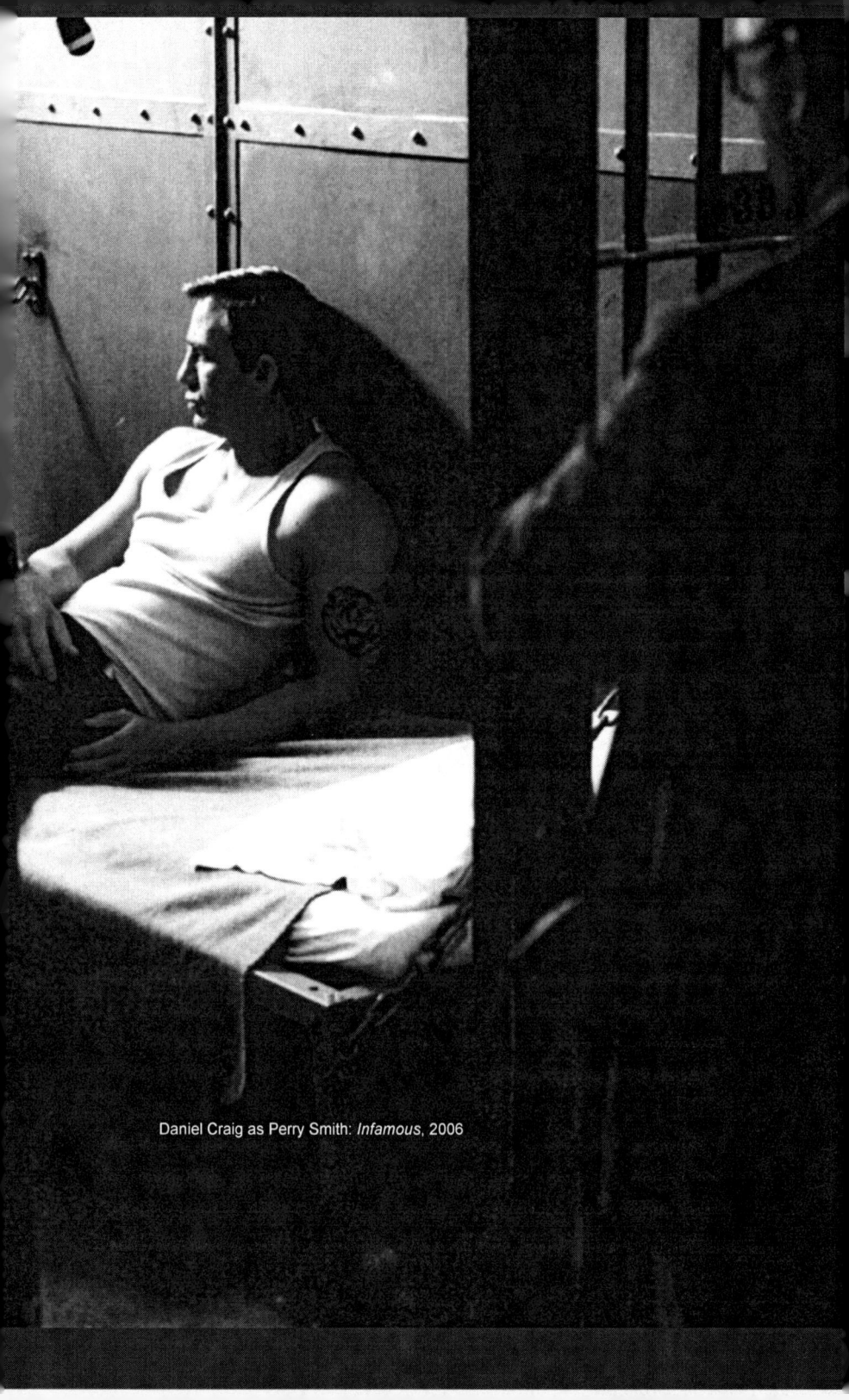

Aging 30 years overnight wasn't easy but the four developed some techniques of their own to look the part, working hard on the set and playing hard off it. 'By episode six last Monday, when we were supposed to be middle-aged, we knew dark circles and bloodshot eyes wouldn't matter,' Daniel told *The Mirror* during filming. Although he isn't known as a party animal – in contrast to some of the women he has been linked with in recent years – others in the industry have since marvelled at his ability to get by on two hours of sleep and still show up in a fit state for work the next morning, having stayed up drinking Guinness all night. 'The only snag was, we had to reshoot the first episode again – and you wouldn't believe how much we'd aged!'

In contrast to the other main parts, Daniel's Geordie was a shady character who goes to work for a London porn king, played by Malcolm McDowell. The series was shot episode-by-episode, except for those featuring McDowell; as he was living in America at the time, the production team didn't want to fork out for any more transatlantic flights than they had to. Whereas the others dabble in superficially more respectable jobs and local politics, Geordie's life descends into drug-dealing, arson, imprisonment – on McDowell's behalf – and homelessness.

Although Geordie was a compelling character, it would be invidious to single out any individual member of the core cast. Geordie may have caught the popular sentiment better than the others, but Gina McKee and Christopher Eccleston were the ones later BAFTA nominated for their performances (McKee won the award for Best Actress in 1997). Of course, McDowell was the real draw in terms of viewing figures; casting him was a real coup for the BBC, which paid off in spades for the other budding hopefuls.

With such an ambitious project there is a lot of room for mistakes. Not only was it a huge strain on the BBC's budget and resources, there had been serious concerns about legal issues. Because the series played heavily on political sleaze, scandal and events from the lives of actual people, there was a risk of action from affected parties. In the end, though, the care and effort made with the script and characters paid off. It was a runaway success from the very first episode. The *Observer's* Ian Bell wrote, 'Flannery's script is faultless; funny, chilling, evocative, spare, linguistically precise. The four young friends about to share 31 hellish years in the life of modern Britain are excellently played.' The British Film Institute described it as a 'powerful and evocative drama series... viewers were gripped because, for all their flaws, [the characters] cared about what happened to their friends. The series impressed with its ambition, humanity and willingness to see the ambiguities beyond the rhetoric.'

As a vehicle for his now upwardly-mobile career, Daniel couldn't have hoped for better. Even today, critics rate the show as one of the greatest BBC series ever made. *Loader* called it 'one of the great barnstorming TV performances of the last 15 years.'

The boost came at exactly the right moment for Daniel, who was flat broke and almost at his wits' end. 'I remember having to plead with the BBC to give me my pay cheque for *Our Friends In The North*,' he told *The Mirror*. It was December 1994, not long after his separation from Harley, and times were hard. 'Christmas was coming up, the bank had eaten my card, my chequebook had been disqualified, I had absolutely no money – yet I had started this amazing series,' he remembers. 'I was so desperate, I actually had to chase the cheque around the BBC office to get it signed. It was ridiculous.' But even with such a prestigious role in the bag, it would still take a while to dig himself out of the hole that two years with only sporadic work had got him into. 'And then, when I paid it into my bank account, it only just cleared my overdraft. I have nothing to show for it. It all went on paying off debts – but that's me. I don't handle money well.' Fortunately for him, money was something he would never have to worry about again. *Our Friends in the North* had ensured that Daniel was going to be hot cinematic property for a long time to come.

Filming the series wasn't just a good career move. It was also fun, a chance to spend some quality time with friends and stretch himself as an actor. One of his favourite stories from his time on the set was how he managed to destroy a Rolls Royce in a scene with Benny Barratt (McDowell) in the back. 'They asked me to spin the wheels on this gorgeous soft-top Rolls and roar out of Battersea power station,' he told *The Mirror*. 'I floored the accelerator, and as I did, I left the bottom of the car behind! The guy who was looking after the car just crumpled – but the producer was over the moon with the shot. And there was Malcolm in the back, going: "Slow down, slow down!" He was terrified.'

That wasn't all. When the series aired early in 1996, it had another strange effect on the public – one that the hapless Daniel was utterly unused to, if the anonymous indictments by his former classmates at the Guildhall were anything to go by. A few years earlier – at least, according to the *Daily Mail* – he was a geeky, greasy-haired loser. Somehow in the following years he had managed to transform himself into a national sex symbol. In fact, so impressed were the viewing public that he received more than 500 letters from fans every week over the course of the series. As well as the usual expressions of appreciation for his acting skills, there were plenty of marriage proposals and offers of the more transient kind. Not bad, given that his character ends up a grubby tramp. Geordie would remain close to the public's heart for a long time afterwards. 'I've had people burst into tears over me, and I'd have to say "Look, Geordie's fine, he's okay, at the end he just walked off, he's quite all right,"' he later said.

'I really am enjoying getting all this mail,' Daniel told *The Mirror* in 1996. No doubt it was another huge boost to his ego. 'It makes me happy that people are enjoying me so much. I get women of all ages writing to me – teenage girlies to older women – and they're from all over, not just the North. One told me it was her first fan letter since she wrote to Mick Robinson from *Magpie* 20 years ago.'

Daniel – described as a 'cross between Jerome Flynn and a pit bull terrier' – was a strange choice of male pin-up for the women of 1990s Britain. All the same, he seemed to find a space in the hearts of thousands of viewers, many of whom took the time to write. 'They're all really nice. They say things like: "I've never seen you before – where have you been all my life?" and "I want to spend the rest of my life with you." A lot of them just have a fetish for the long hair I have in the series. I haven't received any knickers yet, but I guess it's only a matter of time!'

This was clearly a new experience, and one he wasn't entirely sure whether he should cultivate or not. 'I don't know if I'm that sexy,' he claimed. 'I certainly don't encourage it.' But it is equally obvious that he liked to look after himself and enjoyed his status. 'I used to work out a lot and take a pride in my body. But I stopped exercising and lost a lot of weight for my part as Geordie, because the character hits the bottle and has to look emaciated. The only problem is that now we've stopped filming, I just can't get my physique back.' Although he had made a habit of choosing roles that would challenge him as an actor, he still admitted having a weakness for the ones that made him look good. 'I like playing sexy roles. They're always the best.'

Moll Flanders

He wouldn't be disappointed with his next part. This time, it was ITV who hired him for their steamy adaptation of Daniel Defoe's 1722 thriller, *The Fortunes and Misfortunes of Moll Flanders* ('17th Century Fox'). Filming took place over a period of 11 weeks – a fairly lengthy time for a four-hour period drama. Daniel would quickly tire of doing costume dramas after this and would do his best to avoid them in the future.

He was playing alongside Alex Kingston (of *ER* fame). In a time when poverty and lack of opportunity held her back, the social-climber Moll used every trick she could think of (often involving her body) to gain advantage. Daniel's part was that of James 'Jemmy' Seagrave, her one true love among five husbands – one of whom is also her half-brother. When Moll returns to England after a trip to the New World, she tries to attract a wealthy husband by posing as a lady herself. Instead, she runs across Daniel, a bankrupt highwayman who is trying the same ploy to snare himself a rich wife. Their on-off and stormy relationship was a major factor in keeping a large audience of viewers hooked. *Our Friends in the North* was making Daniel into a sex-symbol and ITV made sure they capitalised on that.

Alex Kingston remembers filming the bedroom scenes with Daniel and others. 'The men I had to do the sex scenes with were more tense than me,' she said. 'But we just had a laugh. There would be times when I'd say we needed to see more of the actor's buttocks. So I'd just rip the sheet off his back. I had no inhibitions because it wasn't gratuitous. Moll was an earthy, normal woman who enjoyed sex as much as anybody else.' It didn't hurt Daniel's growing reputation as a northern hunk, either.

Despite his virile appeal, the producers found that Daniel wasn't quite as brave as his character. This would be a recurring accusation in later films (particularly – and predictably – in *Casino Royale*, where critics would suggest he just didn't have the guts to act the role convincingly). In *Moll Flanders*, the story goes that he was too scared to climb onto his horse. In the end, the props manager had to give him a piggyback to give him the extra height he needed for those scenes.

When the series aired in December 1996, the women's magazines knew nothing of this cowardly streak and, for a while, he was a regular feature. But all of the new press activity wasn't appreciated by Daniel. Media interest is an almost inevitable side-effect of a successful acting career, but it was something he was becoming increasingly concerned about and ever more intent on resisting. *Moll Flanders* marked the end of an era for him. After that, he stopped doing any personal interviews. In the decade that has followed, many journalists have tried to encourage him to open up about his private life for the benefit of their readers, only to find that they might as well be trying to get blood out of a stone. He simply refuses to do any lifestyle press – a complete rarity in an industry that thrives on narcissism and self-promotion, and only partly because that kind of publicity also raises viewing figures. 'He's strangely ego-less for an actor,' said one of his friends recently – director John Maybury, who would soon work with him in *Love is the Devil*, 'and able to distance himself from the rigmarole and the palaver of celebrity.'

'He's never taken the easy route,' said actor Nick Reding, in an interview with *The Independent*. 'The road less travelled is what interests him. It's part of his nature, but it's what makes him such a good actor as well.' This trait might be construed by some as the aloofness that some people apparently attributed to him at school. In fact, his friends confirm a very different reality: it is simply that his priorities lie elsewhere. 'The thing about Daniel is he's one of the most evolved people I've ever met,' continued Reding. 'His compassion and his understanding of other people is always spot on. You say one tiny thing to him and he gets it immediately. He's one of the nicest people on the planet, without any question.' Hardly the picture of an anti-social misfit. His reserve is not a sign of arrogance but simply a disengagement from the egocentric trappings of the celebrity lifestyle. His manner isn't the indication of a head stuck in the clouds, but of someone firmly grounded in the real world.

Director Matthew Vaughn (*Layer Cake*) confirms that the actor has pretty down-to-earth tastes. 'When I met Daniel, I thought, "Oh Christ is he going to be a real luvvie thespian? But after ten minutes I discovered that we're both Harry Potter fans and our idea of a good evening is being left alone with a PlayStation.'

After *Moll Flanders,* the only interviews Daniel did were about his work – and he was reluctant to give even those. His personal life was a closed book from then on (though he has recently admitted that's now likely to be practically impossible to maintain). 'I don't go along with this thing that it's part of the job,' he told *The Independent* in 1996, conceding that he didn't find it an easy ideal to live up to. 'It's not the reason I got into this game. I have to be quite guarded, I like to talk and I like people, I'd probably be a tabloid journalist's dream. Get enough drinks down me and I'd tell all.'

Press difficulties would rear their head again, but right now life was good. The number of offers he was getting for all kinds of work meant that he was at the enviable stage of being able to pick and choose what he did. With the world at his feet, he decided to follow his boyhood dream and focus on cinema. Daniel would still do the occasional TV show, and theatre if it was challenging and interesting enough, but the big screen was where his real ambition lay. 'As far as I am concerned, I want to be nowhere else. It's difficult in film because everybody wants to make a safe bet with roles. But if you are going to do stuff, then you should be getting strong reactions. I do not want my audiences just to be going, "Yeah, that's about right", you know?'

Obsession

After *Moll Flanders* wrapped, most of the rest of 1996 was spent filming a German-French production called *Obsession*. If anything displayed his career intentions, it was this move; after his recent critical and popular successes he could have chosen far better paying opportunities than a foreign art film. But that wasn't what motivated him as an actor. 'I don't look at things that way,' he told *The Independent*. 'The script came along and it was a good script, and it meant Berlin for three months, then we went to France, then to Paris, I wasn't going to turn down an opportunity like that – plus it's quite a good movie.'

His father, Tim, has commented on this relative disinterest in financial gain. 'He is his own man and he's not driven by money. I know he has turned down serious cash to do other roles. He tells me that he's turned the parts down because he could never see himself standing up there and saying the words.'

The last year or so had been an incredible rise from near-obscurity to the kind of fame that few actors can hope for. It was particularly poignant given that the two years before that had been so demoralising: a rocky career that was in danger of going nowhere, near bankruptcy and a failed marriage. Daniel wasn't sure what to make of it all. 'I'm bewildered. I don't know what it all means,' he told *The Independent* in 1996, talking about what motivated him and where he hoped to go in the future. 'I think in the end it's all about "Could you show this to your mates?" I would like to think I could sit down with my mates and see something I've done and they'd say "Yes, you've got away with that, that's okay". And if that happens, that's cool.'

Daniel Craig with current lady Satsuki Mitchell, 30th June 2007

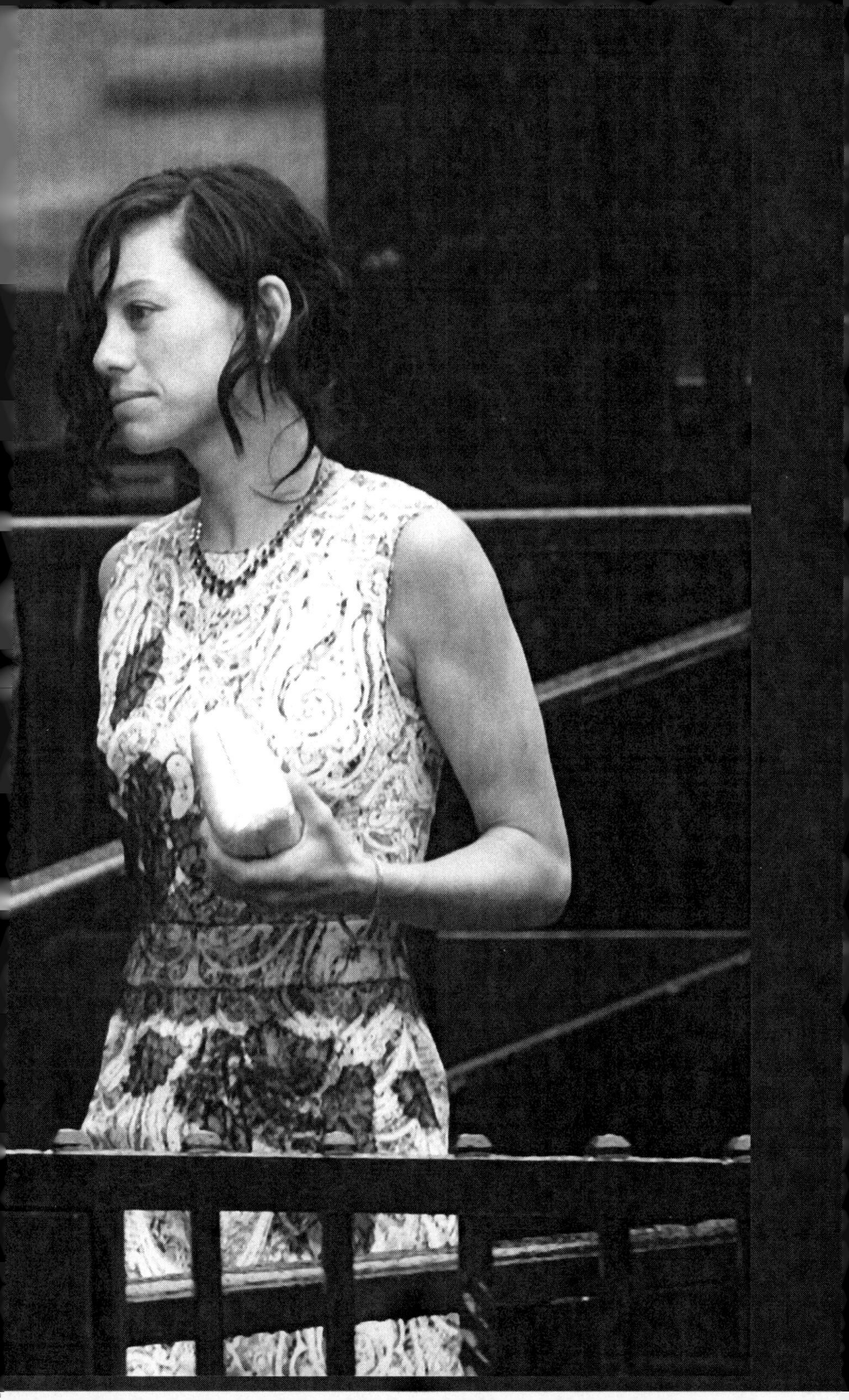

He also admitted that his new life could be a little disconcerting. Acting isn't routine, nine-to-five kind of work; it consists of bursts of intense activity, often for 12 hours a day or more, at least six days a week. Then there is typically a lull when nothing happens, perhaps for months. 'I try and just get my head together when I'm not working. I don't use my time particularly well, I'm not organised, when I've got enough money I'll employ someone to look after me, which is a pretty pathetic actory thing to say,' he said. 'Financially I'm hopeless, completely numerically dyslexic – that's another actor's whine. I quite fancy running clubs actually, but I don't think it'll ever come about, it's a lot of organisation – and finance. I'd lose everything!'

It was also on the set of *Obsession* that he would meet the German actress Heike Makatsch, going on to have a long-term relationship with her. Heike was at about the same stage in her career as Daniel. She had risen to fame in Germany as the star of music channel Viva (a German version of MTV). Widely recognised as a pretty face without much substance, she surprised the viewing public when, in 1996, her first film (*Männerpension*) came out. Since then her career has headed in a very different direction. She managed to cross over to mainstream success in the English-speaking market with her role as the predatory secretary Mia in Richard Curtis' *Love, Actually*. The two would stay together for seven years, eventually breaking up in 2004, just before rumours of Daniel's relationship with Kate Moss hit the headlines.

After *Obsession*, Daniel starred in the political allegory *Love and Rage*, set in 19th century Ireland, and the more mainstream *Elizabeth*. In this last film, about the protestant Queen Elizabeth I's rise to the throne after the death of the catholic Mary, he would be reunited with Christopher Eccleston, his *Our Friends in the North* co-star. Daniel played John Ballard, an evil Jesuit priest. *Elizabeth* later won a mass of awards, including an Oscar.

Love is the Devil

Although Daniel had risen to fame as a northern sex-symbol, he had always supplemented the projects that required this image with others that would ensure he never got pigeon-holed in those roles. His next film, the art house biopic *Love is the Devil,* was a complete departure from any of the films he had done since *Our Friends* pushed him into the spotlight.

The film was an exploration of the private life of the painter Francis Bacon, loosely based on Daniel Farson's 1993 biography *The Gilded Gutter Life of Francis Bacon*. In particular, it focused on the gay relationship Bacon had with George Dyer, a petty criminal whom Bacon surprises when Dyer burgles his flat. ('Take your clothes off and come to bed. Then you can have whatever you want,' says Bacon, a line that works better than might have been expected.) Daniel's image as a rough, northern, working-class character made him perfect for the role. However, filming was extremely tough, both physically and in terms of what was expected from him as an actor. It didn't help that the low-budget film had to be shot in the span of only a month; there was no time to explore Dyer's characterisation with Maybury or ask questions about how he should play the part. 'The role of George Dyer was pretty thankless,' said director John Maybury. 'It was the least well-written because so little is known about him, apart from the John Deakins photographs, but Daniel managed to invest him with a real depth that wasn't in my screenplay.'

In the initial casting, Daniel thought he would again be working with an actor he knew and respected from his earlier days. 'Malcolm McDowell was originally going to play Bacon and I'd agreed to do it with him because John had watched *Our Friends* to see Malcolm and saw me in it, too,' he told the *Daily Record*. 'But then Malcolm, for his own reasons, decided not to do it. I wasn't sure whether to stick with it, but I decided that it would be quite an experience, so I threw myself into it.' In the end, the part of Bacon would be played by veteran actor Derek Jacobi, perhaps most famous as TV's detective monk Brother Cadfael.

In the movie, Bacon is depicted as an unpleasant genius who grows increasingly weary of his new lover's inability to deal with the curious form of celebrity he enjoys. Dyer, despite his rough exterior, is thrown into a world he is not used to and cannot understand. Eventually, he has a breakdown and commits suicide. 'What was always on my mind was getting to the relationship that existed between Bacon and Dyer,' said Daniel. 'In some ways it's like a straight relationship, but I wanted to get to the truth of it. The

2: CRAIG STEPS INTO THE LIMELIGHT… RELUCTANTLY

film is unrelenting, by no means easy to watch, but it was fantastic to do.'

It marked a dramatic departure for him in that the role demanded graphic scenes of Bacon's sadomasochistic sexual relationship with Dyer, including full-frontal nudity. The part required long periods of standing around almost naked, dressed in Y-fronts at the most and smeared in surgical sealant for the S&M scenes. 'There were a couple of days where I had to stand around stark naked the whole time, covered from head to toe in this sticky red stuff to represent one of Bacon's paintings,' he recalled. 'I couldn't do anything. I just had to stand there because if I sat down I'd have stuck to the chair. That was the point where I was at my lowest physically, because I was so knackered. It takes it out of you, but you have to get on with it.'

Although this material was physically tiring, it was easier emotionally than the rest of the film, when he had to interpret what little was known of Dyer and create the rest of the character from the gaps. 'People always say that the stuff I did must have been difficult, but I say it wasn't really – it was in fact some of the easier stuff to do, because it was always clear and made a lot of sense. But when things are unclear and you don't know what you're doing, now that's when things are difficult,' he said.

He has spoken on several occasions about the problems in filming sex scenes, both in this film and in those he has had with women. In the industry, they tend to be treated as simply another day of work, at least by the professionals. 'The sex is taken out of it very, very quickly,' he said. 'You're on a cold and windy set with somebody who you know, and it takes ages so you sit there with a cup of tea smoking a cigarette and talking about the weather, and it just becomes banal. On the whole, sex scenes are pretty boring.'

Maybury, for one, was impressed at the way Daniel had risen to the challenge. 'He brings an incredible stillness and complexity to his roles,' the director said. 'He reminds me of Steve McQueen.' Maybury would later go on to work with Daniel again in the 2005 drama *The Jacket*. 'Craig... creates a poignant figure from the sexy lout whose destiny to be discarded is predicted early on by his roughneck friends,' wrote *Variety's* David Rooney. 'The bluntly handsome Craig, a sort of Cockney James Dean, perfectly captures the confusion and desperation of an uneducated, neurotic, petty criminal more at home with boxers than with artists,' said another reviewer. *Love Is The Devil* was going to open doors for him in the future.

'You make your own decision about how far you want to go, but the best acting is seeing the character out of control, with the actor in total control,' Daniel said about the way he approached the role. The result of that gruelling month was a masterpiece of cinema that would throw a very different light on him as an actor. Aside from demonstrating his range and capability, it prepared the way for other, more challenging parts and showed him as a rising talent who was unafraid to try something new. It also marked the beginnings of his status as a gay icon.

Daniel was steadily growing in reputation as an actor capable of delivering convincing performances that spanned the complete range of emotion – quite a rarity, even amongst the best in the industry. William Boyd, the director in his next film, *The Trench* (another low-budget movie, this time a war drama set just before the Battle of the Somme), recalls his own reaction to the star after filming one of his favourite scenes. Daniel, playing Sergeant Telford Winter, tries to give one of his men a taste of his wife's home-made jam. When the soldier resolutely refuses, even after Winter has pushed the jar at his face, he slumps back into his seat and angrily eats the jam himself, though its homely associations have been ruined for him. 'He has an amazing ability to express emotion of the most poignant kind as well as the most vehement kind,' said Boyd, clearly as impressed as Maybury had been. 'Not all leading men have that – they can do the tough stuff, but they can't always do both.'

This versatility was attracting directors throughout the UK, although Daniel had yet to achieve mainstream success in the international market. That would change very soon. One of his last projects before his 'breakthrough' role to the US was in *Some Voices*. This time, he would be playing a schizophrenic recently released from a mental hospital, who wreaks havoc at his brother's restaurant in London. Once again his early days in *Our Friends* would pay off handsomely; he would be working with Simon Cellan Jones, who directed the series, though this would be his film debut. Daniel had coveted the role for a while, but hadn't felt confident – or arrogant – enough to put himself forwards for it. 'He has scripts lying around and you can't go, "Ooh, can I be in it?" That's not the way friendships work,' he said. 'I said, "I'll just have a look at it and see what I think," so that I could talk to him about it purely on a friendship level. I really just wanted to keep it like that. Finally he said: "I really want you to play it." Fine. Let's do it.'

As an adaptation of a stage play, *Some Voices* appealed to Daniel for the challenges it represented. The story relies heavily on the lead actors, who are on screen almost continuously. There was no room for a poor performance. Ray is borderline insane and dangerous, and this repressed madness was hinted at splendidly by his characteristic restraint. Critically the film was well-received too, with Daniel winning Best Actor at the Independent Film Awards.

The film had its lighter moments, too, such as running down London's Goldhawk Road starkers. 'The scene was written as me running down the road stripped to the waist covered in tomato juice,' he remembers. 'Then I got drunk at Simon's and said, "I'll do it naked!" Never get drunk with directors.' (He has since vowed to lay off the alcohol around directors.) Knowing the risk of charges of indecent exposure, Simon arranged with the local policemen to take a well-timed tea-break. Even then, Daniel admits being scared witless by the prospect; even some Dutch courage didn't help. 'On the day I had to have four large brandies – they didn't touch the sides at all. People just got on with it though. It didn't gather a crowd!'

What *Some Voices* did attract was American audiences. Now with a strong catalogue of roles to showcase his art, he was beginning to gain the respect of directors and film bosses on the other side of the pond. In fact, it is quite likely that this would have happened much earlier, had he not concentrated on the low-budget art-house films that he loved doing. If he had capitalised on his earlier heartthrob status and followed it up with more of the same, it is entirely likely that he would have been gracing Hollywood's silver screen already, and collecting the pay cheques to go with them. Instead, he chose artistic integrity, secure in the knowledge that the roles were there for the taking and that he could pick and choose in such a way as to develop his career in whatever direction he wanted – which was most important to him.

'I know what I'm like with money, and I also know what I'm like with boredom,' he said. 'And I know that being on a long film would just bring out the worst in me. I don't want to do work that's about getting a house in Portugal. Money's obviously an issue and it's nice to have it, but I've tried to go for the jobs which are the most interesting available.'

Also released in 2000 were *I Dreamed of Africa* – a safari film starring Kim Basinger – and *Hotel Splendide*.

His reactions to shooting these two films neatly encapsulate what motivates and inspires him in his choice of movies. After the first, he was decidedly unimpressed; for all its big-budget appeal, it was entirely undemanding. 'I played a part in it which I could do standing on my head, but is still a small part in a big film. You just think, what's the point of doing that? I'd rather do something that I really believe in here that only gets seen by ten people,' he told the *Evening Standard*. There is a real problem that so much of mainstream cinema caters to a lowest common denominator, and as a result can be vacuous and boring to make. *Splendide,* a story of a remote island spa centre, was better; although he was unconvinced to start with, at least it was fresh ground. 'I just read the script and went, I have no idea what this is about, I don't know how I feel about the film. When you take risks they can go two ways. It's a really weird wonderful film and, as a piece of British gothic cinema, it stands alone. But I don't know really what it amounts to.'

'It's a weird piece,' he said. 'But I like weird. Weird is good. Mainstream is crap – even though I'm in *Tomb Raider*.' At least, *Splendide* had artistic integrity. The year 2000 though would be the last time that he would be able to take a part in a film and have the luxury of being able to agonise over whether it was too strange to attract many viewers. From now on, his growing weight as an actor meant that he would no longer be able to experiment.

All actors and actresses have at least one cinematic skeleton in their closet. Perhaps it is an embarrassing childhood commercial or a particularly cringe-worthy part in a straight-to-video movie. Among actresses, there is a tradition of revealing photos suddenly materialising. In Daniel Craig's case, the embarrassing secret is actually what made him an international star.

Tomb Raider began shooting in July of 2000. It was the last thing that anyone would have expected an actor of Daniel's calibre and CV to be interested in. The film – which is one of very few successful computer game-to-movie adaptations – is essentially a vehicle for Angelina Jolie, who jumps, swings, shoots and fights her way through a 100-minute-long plot-light extravaganza of special effects. It was a popcorn movie of the highest order – one that had cinemas packed to bursting with empty-headed fans looking for a way to kill an evening without taxing too many brain cells.

He had been offered the part of Alex West, Jolie's rival and ex-boyfriend. *Tomb Raider* was the highest-grossing film ever with a woman in the lead role – grossing over $270 million worldwide – very different to the kind of fare Daniel was used to. He was far happier working on low-budget art-house flicks with real substance to the parts. So what happened?

'I like action films as much as anybody else,' he told the *Evening Standard*. 'I just thought, well why not? Does it stop me making films that I believe in, or does it raise my profile a little bit so that I might have more choice? It could screw things up, I could have sold my soul to the devil. But I'm doing it happily.' Although he claims that he never regretted *Tomb Raider*, it is clearly something he is uncomfortable about. Later, he would admit that his reasons for taking the part were mostly about the money (with a budget of $80 million, there was plenty of it flying around), although it was nice to see how things were done at the other end of the scale. 'If you're doing things for the money and you're unhappy when you're doing it, you've only got yourself to blame. It's a huge movie: a lot of acting in a vacuum against a blue screen, but the most amazing sets you've ever seen,' he observed later.

Despite the pay cheque and other fringe benefits such as working with Angelina Jolie, it was hardly worth the trouble. 'I thought I'd got myself into something that I didn't understand,' he told *Contact Music*. 'I didn't realise I wouldn't be able to do my job as I saw it, and those films by their very nature stop you acting. You are going to do one line again and again, and the line be something like, 'Watch out!' I just don't think I can do it very well. I need to know more.'

He would later voice his misgivings to *The Independent*. 'I've been on this for six months, and I've got maybe four pages of dialogue, but I do get thrown about a lot and blown up,' he complained. 'I don't know how satisfying that is. I'm waiting to see what the results are, but it isn't the same as coming out of a great scene with great actors and pages of brilliant dialogue, where you feel you've nailed something emotionally – that's a different thing altogether.' Something, he added, 'Which I want to get back to – soon!'

CH 3

REDEMPTION FROM THE LIMELIGHT IN PERDITION

Ironically, for all its faults, it actually took something as superficial as *Tomb Raider* to get international audiences really sitting up and taking notice of him. Vowing he would never sell out for mindless appeal and the big bucks again, Daniel was set for bigger and better things.

'I don't regret for a second doing it but it just wasn't an experience that was that satisfying,' he told *eFilmCritic* of his tomb-raiding experiences. 'I was lucky enough then to go off the next year and do *Road to Perdition*, which cost the same amount of money as *Tomb Raider* but had much more to it – there are only so many ways that you can look surprised at crap blowing up.'

Despite his justification of *Tomb Raider*, it was actually an earlier film that ensured he got the part in *Perdition*. He was offered the role of Connor Rooney, son of a gangster played by Paul Newman, after director Sam Mendes and actor/writer Patrick Marber saw him in *Sword of Honour*. *Sword* was a TV adaptation of an Evelyn Waugh novel set in the Second World War. Marber watched Daniel's portrayal of flawed heroism early in 2001 and told Mendes, 'That's who you want for Connor.'

When Mendes put the idea to Daniel, there was no choice to make. 'There was something like 40 and 50 Oscars on that set, between cast and crew. It was terrifying but I had a word with myself and said "Come on. Get on with it. This will all be over very quickly. If you don't start stepping up to the plate and thinking about it, you're going to be regretting this."'

It was the chance of a lifetime, and one over which he knew he would kick himself for ever if he didn't take it. After the big-studio extravaganza of the past months, it was also a chance to nail his colours to the mast – to show he was happiest in the independent movie scene, despite the problems involved. 'In independent film, you have a freedom with the subject matter,' he said in one interview. 'The ending that you see written in the script may not actually be the one you shoot. There's no debate about "I don't think the audience is going to like this character." Tough shit. We're not asking an audience what they like or dislike. We're trying to move the audience. I don't think movies should always be comfortable to watch. Which is, I think, what I like about this one. This movie goes away from the traditional Hollywood movie. A down ending, I think, is a positive thing, which you don't see very often.'

What it did have going for it was a star-studded cast that had the public slavering before the film even came out. Tom Hanks, who played organised crime 'enforcer' Michael Sullivan, was a big enough lead to pull in the fans on his own, whatever the movie was actually about. Paul Newman played Rooney senior, and Jude Law came into his own as a disfigured, near-psychotic photographer. Despite his fears, working with Hanks and Newman wasn't as big a deal as he thought. 'At rehearsals, I got used to sitting in the same room with them. They're quite down-to-earth. Both so easy to get along with. No bull,' he told the *Chicago Sun Times*.

This was also his first real taste of what life in the glare of the media could be like; when you're as well known as Hanks, a simple evening out becomes impossible. 'You can't really *go out* with Paul Newman and Tom Hanks,' he said. 'I knew Tom was big here, but it gets quite crazy.' He remembers one occasion when they tried to go out for a meal. 'The chef sees Tom Hanks and Paul Newman, and he decides to cook every dessert on the menu. Next thing, there's 32 desserts on the table. It's not good for the diet but, man, it's good.'

Afterwards, it was time to visit some of the more down-to-earth bars that the Windy City had to offer.

'You can't ask Tom Hanks to go to sleazy joints,' he conceded. 'Well, I guess you could, but I wouldn't.' Fortunately Jude Law, who has no such inhibitions, was on hand to take up the slack. 'I like dingy bars,' Daniel said. 'Jude will be recognized once in a while, but we'd put hats on and hunker down, and we'd be fine.' This lack of privacy was one aspect of celebrity he had been able to avoid – so far. Thanks to his unique brand of ambition, he had not risen to fame as fast as his other co-stars in *Our Friends In The North*. Now, it looked like he was going to eclipse them all. 'I've had a very low-key career, to my satisfaction,' he said. 'If I believed everybody who said to me at some point in my career that this was it, I'd be in a mental hospital by now.' But it was getting harder and harder to live his life on his own terms, to finish the day on set and leave his work behind for the evening.

'Acting is ego-based, whether you like it or not,' he admitted in an interview with *The Independent*. 'That's what makes you go out there and do it. But things have got a little bit barmy recently. To tell you the truth, I'm slightly unnerved by the whole thing. And I want to keep as much distance as I can. I try and keep my head down.'

Easier said than done. When *Perdition* came out it was an instant hit, taking $22 million in its opening weekend and confirming that Daniel was capable of taking on mainstream roles just as successfully as the fringe ones he had previously excelled in. It opened Hollywood's audiences to him and immediately made him an international star. There was a strong feeling that he should move out to America to capitalise on his new-found status there, but he was reluctant to leave his life in England behind. 'The truth of it is, that after *Road to Perdition*, I got a lot of good reviews and I could have come over and done a lot of auditions but I just didn't think that was good enough for me,' he told *eFilmCritic*. He had Heike, with whom he shared a flat in London, and his friends and parents to think about. 'I don't think he'll ship out there just yet,' said his mother. 'He is excited about the work but, like the rest of the family, he is pretty non-hysterical about these things. I am just happy to see him doing well in his job and part of that job happens to be that he's famous.'

His father, Tim Craig, was also very proud of his son. After the première of *Perdition*, he told the *Sun* how he had always uncompromisingly encouraged Daniel in his work, even if it meant telling him he hated it. 'I am proud of what he's done but I'm very critical of his acting too. If I don't think it's great I'll tell him straight. I am also proud because he is my mate,' he went on to say. 'I taught him to drink. There's not many things nicer than standing at the bar with someone you love and who loves you that much.'

Daniel's ambition never has quite matched up to the expectations of others; as his friend Nick Reding has said, it is the road less travelled that interests him. 'I have no plans to move over here,' he told the *Chicago Sun Times* on a promotional trip. I'm too old, too cautious. If I was 22, maybe. But I see no point in trying to make my career go better and faster. It's been going OK until now.' It was going better than OK; in just over five years he had gone from a virtual nobody to a transatlantic sensation. There were fantastic opportunities available to him.

He didn't take them. Driven by a desire to keep developing and staying true to his roots, instead he downsized and looked for something totally different (predictably turning down, for example, a reprise of his role as Alex West in the sequel to *Tomb Raider*). One of the next projects he got involved in was a return to the stage, proving he hadn't let fame go to his head. In the same week that *Perdition* premièred, he appeared at London's Royal Court in Caryl Churchill's play *A Number*, also starring Michael Gambon (whose credits include Gosford Park and the part of Dumbledore in the later *Harry Potter* films).

The subject of *A Number*, which ran for eight weeks, was human cloning. Although Daniel and Michael Gambon were the only actors in the play, each was required to act in more than one role. Critics marvelled at the way Daniel was able to play three cloned brothers, giving each of them completely different personalities. *Independent* reviewer Liz Hoggard summed it up as 'the most physically compelling performance I have ever seen'. Daniel concurred: 'It was my dream theatre, an hour long, and then everyone's out in the bar talking about it.'

3: REDEMPTION FROM THE LIMELIGHT IN PERDITION

Tim Craig maintained that his son's performance in *A Number* was just as satisfying to Daniel as his one in *Perdition*, despite the fact that theatre was an apparent step down in the world after Hollywood. 'He's a big fan of Michael Gambon and would have given his left leg to do that stage part,' said Tim. Gambon was just as impressed with his co-star. 'It's a very difficult play. It's very difficult to rehearse, because like all great writing the play gives you so many choices and so much subtext, so we're constantly talking about it.' Daniel's ability to interpret a script and bring it to life – as he had done in *Love Is The Devil* – was again invaluable.

'I've never worked with a young actor so smoothly,' continued Gambon enthusiastically. 'He's so intelligent and sharp and clever. And I'm not just saying that, he's just perfect. He can do anything. We rehearse for hours and hours on end and we try and reach conclusions, and he's very intelligent and sharp and has got it all off pat. He can just sum it all up. I'm an old carthorse, really. A bit lazy. So it's very nice to have Daniel around.'

As if to prove that he really hadn't sold out to the rich studios, a further three projects saw the light of day towards the end of 2002, each completely different, definitely not what could be considered 'mainstream' and all quite unlike his big-screen appearances that year. The first was *Copenhagen*, released at the end of September. This was a film adaptation for BBC4 of another stage play that explored the events around a meeting between two nuclear physicists in 1941 – a meeting shrouded in mystery but one that certainly had something to do with the development of the atom bomb. It was described by Los Angeles' *Daily News* as 'a wonderful mystery within a character study within a painless physics-for-dummies lesson'. Daniel was playing Werner Heisenberg opposite Stephen Rea's Niels Bohr. Quantum mechanics and Nazism may not be the most compelling subjects for a film, but – by now predictably – critics praised his ability to immerse himself in a role. 'English actor Daniel Craig keeps Heisenberg cold and hot at the same time – leaving us wondering again if he is better or worse than he seems,' said one.

Ten Minutes Older: The Cello, released in December, was a collection of 15 short films – each 10 minutes long – on the subject of time. He played a space man who returns after an 80-year flight at near-light speed to find he has aged only 10 minutes. *Occasional, Strong*, a 12-minute-long gangster story that owed a lot to *Lock, Stock and Two Smoking Barrels*, was released on the same day.

Bigger Fish

It wasn't just filming that was keeping him busy – although he had two other major films on the go in 2002. His close friend, Nick Reding, had decided to take a break from acting and set up a new charity, SAFE – 'Sponsored Arts For Education' – a Kenya-based theatre project designed to educate people about HIV and AIDS. After 20 years as a self-proclaimed 'jobbing actor', he realised that he wanted more from life, despite the fact that offers for major parts were rolling in now. Daniel hates self-promotion, but this was a cause close to his heart (he had, after all, been wrapped in a copy of *The Guardian* at birth) and he put his weight behind it with a series of promotional interviews. 'Nick did the thing all of us maybe plan to do eventually, when we sort ourselves out. Because at the back of every actor's mind there's the thought: "Is this where I'm going to be for the next 20 years? Maybe there's an adult job out there for me, one that doesn't involve all of this shit,"' he told *The Observer*, hinting at dissatisfaction with film-making in his characteristic self-deprecating way. 'His support of SAFE has been invaluable to us,' said Reding, 'and his support to me, as a best friend, as I've taken this journey, has been probably even more valuable.'

The Mother

When he wasn't acting in surreal short films or promoting SAFE in 2002, Daniel was spending quality time with a naked 68-year-old woman. His next film, the controversial *The Mother*, was directed by *Notting Hill's* Roger Mitchell. Summarised as 'a damning portrayal of western humanity, which runs the risk of being as hollow and callous as the people it portrays, but the cast give heart to the hopelessness,' it deals with the touchy subject of a man's affair with his girlfriend's mother. The film required explicit sex scenes with pension-aged actress Anne Reid. 'Mainly, the film is about broken families and how they hardly talk to each other – that is the crux of the movie,' he said. 'It is really complicated with this film about an older woman whose husband dies and she has an affair where everything ends horribly.'

'It disturbed me,' he told the *Evening Standard*. 'I didn't feel sympathy for any of the characters. In the wrong hands it could have been coy, it could have been awful.' As it happened, he and Roger Mitchell got on well together as soon as they met and Roger quickly persuaded him to take the part. 'It was a Hanif Kaureishi screenplay and though I am probably kidding myself about it now, I was scared shitless about the script and what it required of me,' he admitted.

'I didn't even want to think about it, to tell the truth. I spoke to Roger on the phone and said, "I don't know if I want to do this. I don't like these people" and he said, "That is why we are making it." Roger is an incredibly charming guy and he knows his stuff, it is as simple as that. He got me involved in making the movie and I love the fact that it is shocking. I love the fact that audiences sometimes say "That movie made me sick!" while others go on a roll with it and saw the dark side.'

Anne Reid appreciated the chance to get to know him better. 'He has plenty of sex appeal,' she conceded. But initially she was as cautious as Daniel about the film's taboo-breaking theme. 'I was frightened out of my mind,' she recalled. 'I rang my son, cried and said, "I can't do it". He just said, "Mother, it's a wonderful part. If you are inhibited it's not going to work."

'I got absolutely paralytic,' she continued. 'But of course on the day I was stone cold sober – you get through anything just like you do when you go to the dentist. You just think, "I have to do this." When it came to it I wasn't embarrassed and made lots of jokes. It was hysteria actually. I'd like to do it again now,' she added, 'with anybody!'

Daniel's own mother's reaction? 'My mother turned 60 this year and she's a very young sexual being,' he recalled. 'I don't know anything about her sex life and I don't want to know. She hasn't seen the film yet but I hope it moves her. And that's not just because I get my butt out.'

Sylvia

His next role did far more for his already substantial sex-appeal; in fact, it relied on it as one of the film's chief themes: a dangerous, compulsive quality, destructive to those around him. Daniel was perfect for the part, though he was almost as nervous about acting in this one as he was about *The Mother*. This time, at least it was a subject he felt passionately about.

The film was *Sylvia* – an exploration of the turbulent relationship between the famous poets Ted Hughes and Sylvia Plath. Ted's affairs, Sylvia's insecurities and depression, the breakup of their marriage and her eventual suicide made for touchy subject matter and demanded careful handling; Daniel, who played Ted, was right to be nervous.

'There's quite a bit of pressure riding on it,' he said. 'And also just the whole shit that goes with it – you know, the hatred directed at Ted Hughes. People are still scrawling "pig" on his grave.' Plath gassed herself in an oven after Hughes left her for another woman.

Still, he hoped he would be able to bring more energy to the part than he had witnessed from the poet himself. 'I mean, bless him, he didn't read poetry particularly well,' he remembered of his hopeful childhood visit to a Hughes reading. 'It was just this monotone crap. "This is called Crow. Crow sits in... duh duh duh... Blood and otters... Birth and death... thank you very much."'

With that in mind, there was definitely some room for artistic licence. 'I didn't want Ted to be an impersonation,' he told *The Independent*. 'I've got hours of tape of his poetry. I've been listening to him for as long as I can remember. But nobody speaks like Ted Hughes any more. His accent is a mixture of Yorkshire-cum-Cambridge-cum London; it's bizarre.' (His own accent had undergone some changes along the same lines in the years that he had been living in London, losing its Scouse twang and morphing into something more mid-Atlantic and audience-friendly.)

'It looks like it's going to be a sad movie, but what can you do about that?' The Plath/Hughes story is depressing material at the best of times and it didn't help that Gwyneth Paltrow, who played Sylvia, had just lost her father. 'That brings a reality into it,' he told

The Guardian. 'It was very upsetting. I don't think the filming process itself was upsetting – it was just too big a deal. I don't know how she coped really. She did brilliantly. And her mum was there, Blythe Danner. She plays Plath's mum in the movie.'

Alongside the sadness and emptiness of the film, reviewers picked up on the intended 'smouldering' and 'saturnine' sex appeal he brought to the part. 'In Hughes's poems, which are full of violent animal imagery, hawks and crows have a special totemic significance, and Mr. Craig, with his craggy, shadowed face, looks like a rangy, wounded bird of prey,' recorded the *New York Times*. 'His voice is a low growl, and his sexual magnetism, the trait that is the movie's main concern, is palpable.'

'The two young poets meet at a party at Cambridge University. At the end of their first kiss, he steals one of her earrings and she bites his cheek, drawing blood. Later, at a small gathering in period-shabby student rooms, they hurl passages of Shakespeare at each other, then tumble into bed. Sex and poetry are linked in this film as if by a high-tension, high-voltage wire, and while the connection may seem facile, it is also, with respect to these writers and their milieu, entirely plausible.'

Gwyneth Paltrow was the only one not convinced by Daniel's charms. She has admitted being genuinely confused at what so many other women on the set found attractive about him. 'It's so funny, women really like him,' she said, bemused. 'They're really drawn to him sexually. They think he's a smouldering, charismatic, sexy man. People keep commenting on the chemistry between us. But that's acting...'

Daniel has spoken on many occasions about his respect for Hughes. As he is, himself, an intensely private person, he can appreciate the quality in other people. The poet waited almost 40 years to publish *Birthday Letters,* an autobiographical collection of poems about his time with Sylvia. He only did so when he was dying of cancer, which he also kept secret from all but a small circle of those closest to him. 'I respect him greatly for keeping his counsel for all those years,' he told *The Independent.* 'A lot of people thought, "Well, there you go, he might as well have admitted his guilt about killing her," but my heart says no, it's about something far more complicated than that, something we will never know about, something we have no right to know about.' Although Hughes remarried, he admitted in *Birthday Letters* that he never stopped thinking about Plath. Undoubtedly there were other secrets that he took to his grave.

'I don't think doing this film is about uncovering that element. It's about uncovering an incredible moment in world literature, the coming together of these two souls, these two amazing people and the shit that flew,' Daniel continued passionately. 'And the way we moved into the late 1950s, this supposed renaissance of world thinking – the beginnings of feminism, the beginnings of a lot of free thinking, which was incredibly exciting, but incredibly tied down by the rigidity of British society. Sylvia Plath was educated to marry. She was sent to a very good school, but never really to do anything. She had to balance being a perfect home-maker with being an artist and mother. I have a huge amount of sympathy for that because I don't think things really changed a great deal for women until the 1970s.'

He shared Hughes's reticence when asked to voice his own opinion of the poet – much maligned for the way he is seen to have driven Plath to suicide. 'I could not try to recreate that huge legend. He's solid, huge, a block of granite on the moors. But I know what I feel about the man, and nobody can get me on that,' he reluctantly told the *Evening Standard,* pointedly using some of Hughes's own poetic imagery in the process. 'I've read the poetry and I had the conviction that I could do it. He kept his counsel for all those years, and that was the key for me. I wish I had that strength.'

Enduring Love?

His performance was particularly poignant for him because, in the same month that Sylvia was released, his own seven-year relationship with Heike Makatsch came to an end. He was, as ever, very low-key about the whole matter, naturally choosing not to discuss it in public. However, this kind of press-free lifestyle was now almost impossible to maintain. Three months later, when he embarked on a short romance with the world's most famous supermodel, he would be given a crash-course in dealing with unrelenting media speculation and intrusion. This was the last time he would be able to call his private life truly private. All things considered, it was amazing that he had managed to last so long.

Having proven himself as a smouldering sex-symbol for women, his next move helped him corner the gay market. *Enduring Love* was an adaptation of a bestselling Ian McEwan novel that dealt with the theme of stalking. Rhys Ifans (*Notting Hill's* hygiene-deficient 'masturbating Welshman', Spike) played his obsessive fan, Jed.

Thanks to his contempt of the spotlight, Daniel had never had to deal with his own stalker. 'I don't think so anyway,' he told the BBC. 'They're very good if they are there. But I do know people that have stalkers and it's not nice... Some stalkers are quite benign, but finding someone in your garden at three o'clock in the morning with a meat cleaver and a hard-on can't be much fun.'

After the pair witnessed a hot air-balloon accident, in which a man dies, Ifans' character – an overly-insistent misfit and loner – develops a powerful attachment to Daniel's and convinces himself that there is something special between them. And, indeed, at one point in the film they do consummate their specialness, when the dysfunctional Jed contrives to share a kiss with the object of his affections... something that further reinforced Craig's growing status as a gay icon.

ENDURING LOVE

A NOVEL

IAN McEWAN

'I snogged Daniel Craig before any Bond bird got her hands on him!' boasted Ifans. 'He still says, even after James Bond, that getting to grips with my mouth in *Enduring Love* was the hardest stunt he's ever had to do. For me it was a love story and I spent all day winding him up – waiting outside his door leaving little notes, phoning him and asking if he was lonely. I was doing the countdown to the snog scene saying things like, "Only three days left now." We had a scream.'

Daniel managed to take it all in his stride. 'We took the piss out of each other all the way through filming. We were going, "Three days to go. Two days to go..." Rhys was wearing these cracked plastic teeth so it was bizarre when we did it. But it was fine. We filmed it at the end and by the time we got there we were into the groove of things. But it was just a kiss, nothing more. Honest!' It wasn't the strangest thing Ifans has ever locked lips with; he admits '...kissing a fish, while shooting *The Shipping News* in Newfoundland, with Kevin Spacey and Dame Judi Dench. That was pretty weird.'

Perhaps Daniel should have been more worried. Ifans immersed himself in the world of stalkers in an attempt to find the right mindset to bring to the film. 'There's a predatory side in all of us,' he said in an interview with the *Detroit Free Press*. 'It's the rare bloke who can honestly say he's never been so deeply in love with or obsessed by someone who has rejected him that they follow them. I think it's just that most people finally get to a point where they know it's time to pack it in and get on with things. Jed has nothing to get on to.'

'Some people mistake it for a homosexual thing, but it isn't that at all,' maintained Ifans. 'And I never once thought of myself as a character in a thriller. It's just love, without any of the qualifiers or enhancements or excuses. I truly believe this is one of the most beautiful love stories ever made.' His infectious zeal to nail the part bordered on the disturbing at times. He even stalked his own girlfriend for practice, wanting to know what it really felt like. When he told her at the end of a full day of following her every move, he said, 'She felt violated, even though she didn't do anything out of the ordinary – thank God. I'm not sure what I would have done if I discovered she had something going on she had been keeping from me.' He did the same with Daniel – partly as a joke, partly to bring the reality of the part home to both of them. He would loiter outside his co-star's trailer after filming and phone him constantly at any time of day or night. 'It was funny, but it was also unsettling, and I think it was quite clever of him in retrospect. Because I really did, you know, just wish he would go away and let me alone.' When it came to unwinding after a day of this torment, Daniel was more confident. 'There's always a certain amount of emotional residue at the end of the day, but nothing a pint of Guinness can't resolve.'

Mrs Kate Crack-Head

It would take a lot longer than an evening and a lot more than a pint of Guinness to move on from the rumours that would soon follow. This time, the emotional residue came in the form of supermodel Kate Moss.

Daniel met Kate in March of 2004 through one of her close friends, Samantha Morton, who was working with him and Ifans in *Enduring Love*. Daniel had split from Heike only two months earlier and Kate was in a similar situation. She had recently broken up with Jefferson Hack, the father of her young daughter, after a four-year on/off relationship. After Lila Grace's birth in September 2002 Kate had reverted to a string of short-lived relationships. In recent months, she and Hack had been seen together and it was rumoured that they were an item again. Certainly Jefferson appeared to think so. He had never given up hope that Kate might come around and, friends related to the media, had repeatedly asked her to marry him. Kate was having none of it, though, on one occasion humiliating Jefferson in public by scorning the idea of marriage to him.

Jefferson is a curious mix. Although he is sober and respectable – at least compared to some of Kate's other close friends – he is also cool and fashionable. Daniel was quite different, preferring to avoid any publicity and shopping for clothes at Marks and Spencers (corduroy trousers are a favourite). But the cliché 'opposites attract' is apt; despite having totally different lives and priorities, the two hit it off.

Kate's circle couldn't understand what she saw in him. 'A lot of her close friends just can't see it,' the *Daily*

Mail quoted one. 'Jefferson suited her cool, uber-chic image, but Daniel is the opposite. He's rather serious, intelligent, low-key and terribly unglamorous.' Kate is known for her fondness for wild partying, promiscuity and drug-taking. Daniel is known for enjoying a quiet evening in a pub with a few pints.

He may not have been her usual type, but there was clearly something there. 'Kate is drawn to actors, and she was smitten with Daniel from the first time she met him, although he didn't have a clue,' another friend told the *Daily Mail*. 'They started talking about the theatre, as Kate is interested in moving into acting. She was giving him all the signals, but he assumed she was out of his league.' Rumour has it that he even offered her acting lessons to help develop her new craft.

Kate gave him her telephone number and they stayed in contact over the next few months. 'They started having flirtatious conversations. They weren't sexual, just friendly and jocular.' When Kate went on a modelling shoot to New York, Daniel went with her. 'He was a shoulder to cry on when her relationship with Jefferson was crumbling, and so when she was offered a job in New York she thought it would be a good chance to take him and get to know each other better,' said one source. They spent the weekend in a hotel suite together. 'There is a real spark between them,' another told the *Daily Mail*. 'No one knows if it is going to be something that lasts but Kate is very excited.' Not that, as even her friends admit, it takes very much to get Kate Moss excited.

Daniel was obviously acutely aware of the press frenzy that follows Kate everywhere she goes. He did everything he could – unsuccessfully – to make sure they were not seen together on their trip to the Big Apple, including taking separate taxis to the hotel and ordering in room service pizza rather than risk going out for a meal. Paparazzi snapped them at the airport, though, and the cat was instantly out of the bag. 'Both of them were freaked out by being spotted,' a friend related. 'Daniel in particular hates being in the limelight, so he said he'd understand if she didn't want to see him again. That is exactly the right note to strike with Kate. It made her keener on him.'

'She says she's completely smitten, and keeps asking Sadie and Fran what they think of him,' said another source. 'Of course, they're telling her they think he's fabulous, although privately they're bemused, especially as they haven't seen Kate behave like this for a long time.'

Unfortunately for both of them, there was more fallout to worry about than the press coverage alone. Once the story got into the papers, both of their respective exes – previously oblivious – got to know about the new relationship. Jefferson, who had secretly been hoping to start back where he left off with Kate, perhaps even having another child together, was stunned when he found out. 'Jefferson still harboured hopes of a reconciliation, so it was a real blow,' said one friend to the *Daily Mail*. 'He hoped it was just a fling.' Hack's hopes were raised and then dashed when Kate went

3: REDEMPTION FROM THE LIMELIGHT IN PERDITION

out for a romantic dinner with him in the same week that she returned from New York, only to continue seeing Daniel.

Perhaps Jefferson knew Kate well enough not to expect any better, but Heike was another story. She, too, had apparently held out hopes that they would get back together. 'To say the news about Kate came as a shock is an understatement,' said a friend. 'Heike had no idea he was seeing Kate and felt that he should at least have warned her. She feels let down.'

Heike read about the couple in *The Mirror* at the beginning of April. 'Heike is furious that Daniel has run off with Kate. After seven years together, she hoped he would at least have warned her. She had no idea that he had started seeing her. To say it came as a bit of a shock is an understatement. She feels utterly let down and devastated. Heike thought she and Daniel would work out their differences and get back together but there is no chance of that now – she thinks Daniel has been spineless and cruel.'

'Even though they split late in January, Heike had still been holding a candle for Daniel. They had kept in touch – but he certainly never mentioned Kate. Heike's been in bits ever since. It's bad enough losing the love of your life, but she feels stabbed in the back too. Heike is throwing herself into her work but she is still extremely angry. She feels that Daniel has been very underhand.'

Daniel Craig and Nicole Kidman: 79th Annual Academy Awards, Los Angeles, 25 February 2007

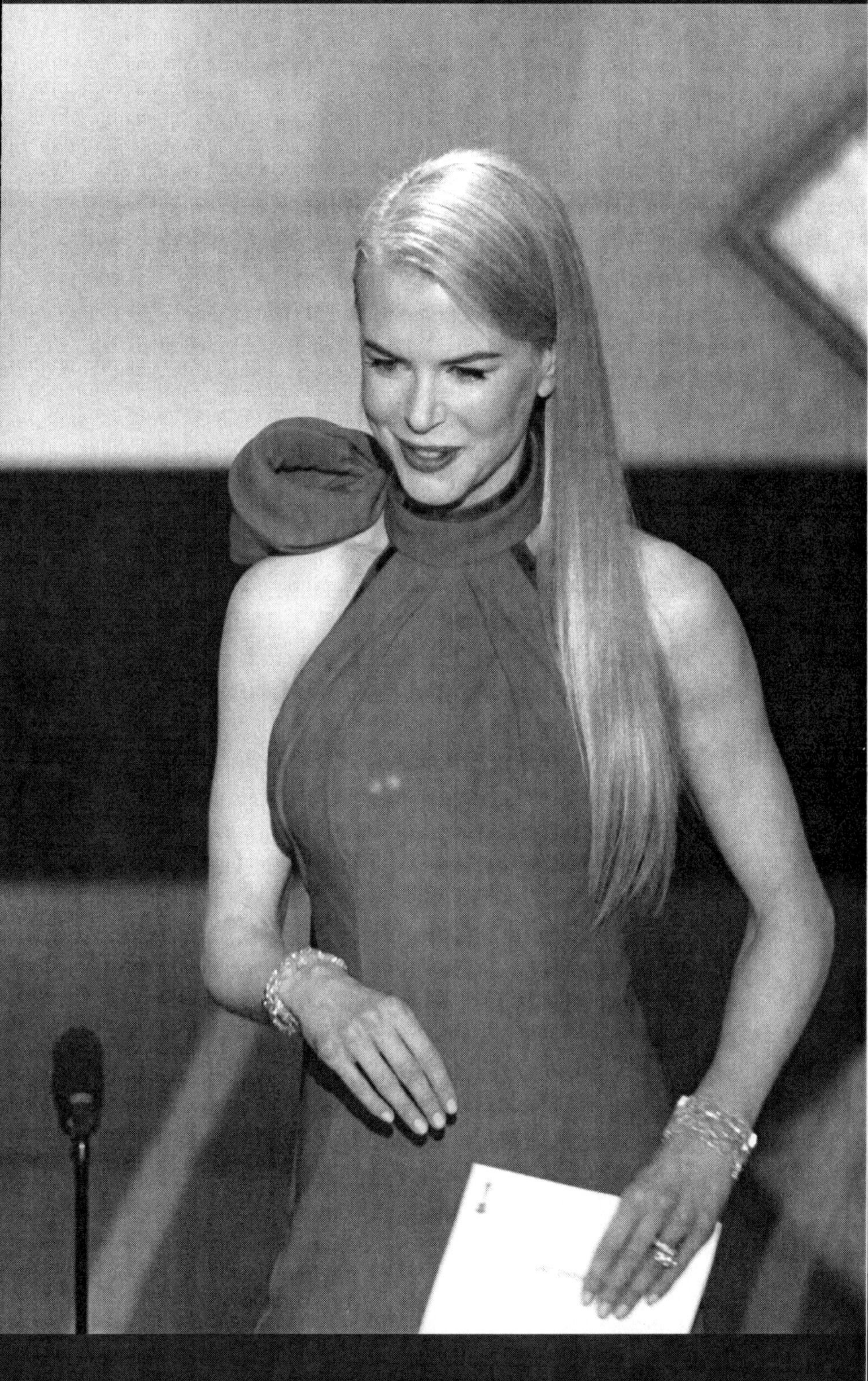

Daniel was dismayed by all the attention. Kate, though, was said to be 'besotted'. As the rumour-mill ground into action, there were soon suggestions of an imminent engagement and headlines of 'Mrs Potato Head'. 'It was love at first sight for Kate,' one friend told the *Sunday Mirror*. 'Daniel is bright, charming and leads a very low-key life – just what Kate's looking for at the moment.' They should have known better. No one linked with Kate Moss leads a quiet life. 'It is serious, and they both know it. Kate doesn't want anything to rock the boat. She is blown away by him. Only her closest friends were in on the secret. They all think he is utterly gorgeous. Both he and Kate want to keep things low-key. But the sexual chemistry between them is so potent that you'd be blind not to see it. Some things you just can't keep quiet.'

Things were getting out of hand very quickly. For all Kate's enthusiasm, Daniel wasn't used to paying this price. The paparazzi and press heat were distasteful and unwelcome in the extreme. One story even suggests he was forced to escape through a restaurant kitchen to get away from photographers. The problem is that Kate just doesn't do low-key, even on the occasions she actually wants to. The relationship fizzled within a few months. Some speculate that Kate's brief fling with Jackass star Johnny Knoxville called time on it, but it is more likely that press intrusion was the deciding factor: it's not what Daniel signed up for. You could forgive him for deciding he couldn't take the tabloid heat and that it was time to get out of 'Cocaine' Kate's kitchen.

3: REDEMPTION FROM THE LIMELIGHT IN PERDITION

'If half the things they wrote about Kate and me had happened it would have been an interesting story but they didn't,' Daniel said on one of the rare occasions he spoke about their relationship. 'It gets twisted,' he told the *Daily Mail*. 'The awful thing about it is, you ask me a question like that, and you print my answer, and then it can hurt people. I know this to my detriment, and I don't want to hurt people.'

What he was really angry about was the way that speculation and often unfounded rumour from dubious sources had an effect on people he cared about – not least, his ex-girlfriend, Heike. 'To get publicity for something like that is unfair on the people in your life. My personal life is totally my personal life and I'll cling to that as aggressively as I can,' he told *Contact Music*. 'I'm not stupid. When it happened to me it wasn't a surprise. But it was incredibly disturbing. I can't imagine anyone enjoying it, and if they do, then I find that quite peculiar.' Despite his caginess, he was willing to answer how Kate's kiss measured up to Rhys Ifans'. 'It doesn't compare,' he said with a rare smile.

Despite the continuous questions that he still gets, even today, about their short-lived relationship, Daniel appears to have got over it all much faster than Kate. In September 2004, his new film, *Layer Cake*, was premièring at the Electric Cinema on Portobello Road in London. Kate hadn't been invited, but turned up to the event anyway. She didn't even manage to meet Daniel, who was busy rubbing shoulders with crowds of other beautiful women.

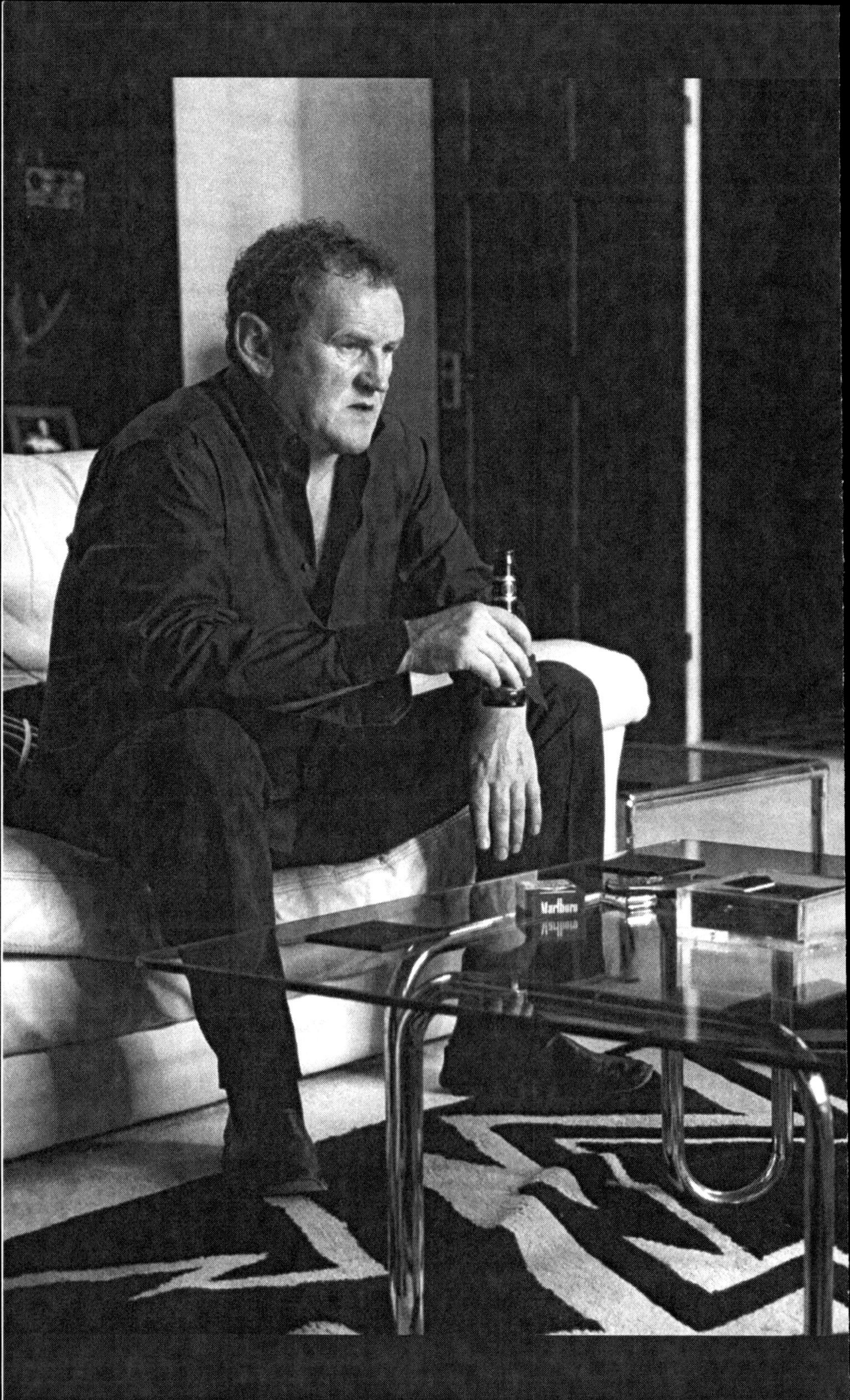
Marlboro

Colm Meaney and Daniel Craig: *Layer Cake*, 2004

'It did seem rather desperate of her to randomly be there,' said *The Mirror's* source. 'She wasn't even invited to begin with. To her credit she didn't try to gatecrash the screening – which was a good job as there wasn't one spare seat in the cinema. Perhaps ringing Daniel up next time she fancies seeing him would be an easier option.' If the 'besotted' supermodel was still holding a candle, it was too late. Daniel had moved on.

Having his Cake

Layer Cake had started shooting the previous year, before all the hype around Kate had blown up. But the film would provide the context for the next round of press speculation that would thwart Daniel in his pursuit of the quiet life.

The main character in the film has no name and is referenced in the credits simply as XXXX. His situation is reminiscent in some ways of Daniel's own. He is presented at the beginning of the movie with none of the history or background information we typically associate with either film characters or celebrities. He just exists, in the present, without past context. For someone who despises attention, that idea had its own appeal. 'This guy rang true to me. We know them or we at least see them in the street every day and we don't notice them because they don't want to be noticed.'

The intelligent thriller – which follows a cocaine dealer in the events leading up to his planned early retirement – was a real challenge, not least in how to form a character without the backstory. 'Method actors suggest that you do sense memory exercises every time you do a scene,' he said – something impossible in this case. 'I use every method I can. Whatever works, I'll use.' The anonymity of XXXX was intriguing. He told *Combustible Celluloid*:

> **Not to be wanky, it's the beauty of the human face. An audience fills it in. Good cinema lets the audience guess all the way through.**

His strategy was to play down the character, presenting him in as neutral terms as possible. 'He would walk into a hotel, walk into the lobby, meet people, talk to people, walk out and no one would notice he was there.'

He was acting alongside Michael Gambon again (on a brief sabbatical from filming the next *Harry Potter* film). His co-star in *A Number* was playing the underworld boss Eddie Temple, the cherry on the top of the layer cake of criminal society. 'It's terrible trying not to laugh because he just makes most of his lines up,' said Daniel of Gambon. 'It's a shot in the dark for him.'

Lock-Stock's Guy Ritchie was initially slated to direct, but when he dropped out Matthew Vaughn took over. Working with Vaughn didn't get off to the best start, though the director soon developed a healthy respect for Daniel. Daniel is often quite hands-on when it comes to filming, frequently having significant creative input into the way scenes are shot. 'I'd watched Guy a lot and Guy is very pedantic about how lines should be read, so he does line reading to the level of telling people where pauses should be and so on,' Vaughn told the *Daily Record*. 'I got told off by Daniel for line reading, which I thought was the normal way of doing it. That was the only faux pas I made!'

'He just asked me things,' Daniel said about working with Vaughn. 'He's not precious about what he does. He asked me questions and if I saw him doing something that I thought wasn't the best way to talk to an actor, I'd go and tell him. And he was like, "Good good! Tell me, tell me, tell me!" He was just so unprecious about his ego.'

Vaughn was certainly pleased with his choice of Daniel as XXXX. *Layer Cake* superficially has the feel of other recent gangster films, but is altogether classier – which is why he wanted Daniel for the part in the first place. 'I didn't want to do another *Lock, Stock and Two Smoking Barrels* and *Snatch*,' said Vaughn. 'I wanted to try and do a film which although it's in the same vein it's a totally different piece and he supported that.'

'It's less of a gangster movie and more of a crime movie,'

said Daniel himself, keen to distance the film from its more violent, crime-glamourising cousins. 'It really does go against the grain as far as gangster movies are concerned. I've had quite a few scripts thrown at me about British gangster movies and they've never appealed to me because ultimately you're standing round in shark suits with sawn off shotguns going, "Come on, you slags!" There is some of that in the movie, but it's only part of a bigger picture.'

Given that *Layer Cake* is about a cocaine dealer, what are Daniel's own thoughts about illegal drugs? 'I think we kid ourselves that people – that governments – don't make huge amounts of money... it's good hard cash. And it's untraceable, that's what people use drugs for, you've got a huge amount of cash and no one knows about it,' he told *Cinema Confidential News*. 'And we kid ourselves about the fact that people don't still use them. And more money can be made off them if they are illegal. The whole system is hypocritical. I think it should be addressed in much more intelligent way, but it won't happen till people stop using them for their own good.'

Daniel is not always the suave, together character he plays so well in some of his films. He talked about one scene in the filming of *Layer Cake* when he is threatened at the top of a high building. 'I don't know how far up we were but we had to climb up eight rickety ladders to get to the top floor so once we were up we had to spend the whole day filming,' he told the *Daily Record*. 'It was terrifying. I've always been scared of heights, but when you've got these butch stuntmen standing around you, you have to get over your terror fairly quickly.' This instinct for self-preservation was again interpreted as cowardice in some circles – particularly when he was rumoured to have been suggested as the latest Bond actor. His fight scenes also fell some way short of the spy's.

'It was a lot of fun having the shit beaten out of me,' he said. 'It was par for the course for this kind of film. At some point you are going to have to fall to the ground and get kicked. But I quite like it though.' Marginally less stressful was the sex-scene he almost shared with Sienna Miller, Primrose Hill Set actress and model, and girlfriend of Jude Law. XXXX is constantly interrupted when he tries to consummate his relationship with Sienna's character, Tammy.

Daniel was full of admiration for his co-star. 'Sienna is special, she has chutzpah. I've heard she's considering giving up because of the pressure – but this is one artist who shouldn't. She's on her way up and is a great actress.'

(Thanks to *Layer Cake* – and the Kate Moss story, which was still playing out – Daniel was about to go stratospheric himself. 'I'm happy talking about my work, but I don't want to be a celebrity,' he said – a statement which would soon turn out to be utterly futile. 'I'm quite shy and it's not for me. If I'm not working I don't want to sit around talking about myself.')

Sienna, on the other hand, was already a dab hand at giving tabloids precisely the kind of raunchy copy they like to print. She told the *Sunday Mail:* 'My character is a pretty steamy, saucy, East End girl. She's fun. Part of me was very nervous about playing someone who is that obviously sexual and slightly tarty but once I got on set, all of those worries disappeared, because it was such a laugh. My first love scene with Daniel was extremely erotic. He's extremely sexy. It was a lot of snogging and sitting on top of him but not starkers. I wore a skirt and top then went to the bathroom and got into knickers, bra and suspenders.'

Unfortunately for Daniel, XXXX was dragged away by gangsters before she could return from the bathroom. 'Daniel just has this incredibly sexy way about him. He's also a very focused actor and very giving,' she said. 'He and Jude are really close friends since they did *Road to Perdition* together and I end up playing both their girlfriends in my two films, *What's It All About, Alfie?* and *Layer Cake.*' That triangle would take on a whole new significance within a year.

'The sex scene with Daniel didn't bother me. I just can't let it,' claimed Sienna. 'If I panicked about it, I wouldn't be able to do it properly. I wasn't naked with him. I've never done a full naked sex scene.'

In contrast Daniel seems to have been more worried about the scene. 'Did I look nervous?!' he asked *Cinema Confidential News*. 'I don't think you can ever really make yourself comfortable when you're doing a sex scene where there are ten people in the room you don't know that well. They're not exactly...sexy.' However, not long after *Layer Cake* premièred, a very sexy rumour began to circulate in the movie world. Early in 2005, the word was that Daniel Craig had been short-listed for the role of the sixth James Bond.

Whilst many of his fans waited with baited breath for a final decision to be made (over 200 actors had been considered to step into Pierce Brosnan's shoes as the spy's latest incarnation), a vocal minority were not impressed and waged a campaign against the casting choice. 'Not a fan of Dan? You are not alone,' proclaimed the movement's dedicated website, www.danielcraigisnotbond.com.

'Millions of James Bond fans are unhappy with Daniel Craig. We do not hate Daniel Craig personally, but we do take James Bond personally,' it continued. 'Daniel Craig's odd looks, lack of charm and sophistication make it undeniable he is wrong for the role.' Despite the fact that the decision had not been confirmed, let alone the movie actually made, the campaign gained momentum among Bond fans, who cited everything from his 'wooden' demeanour to blond hair as reasons he couldn't do the job properly.

Meanwhile, new films were pushing his profile higher than ever. Whilst the publicity was great for his career, he was finding his low-key lifestyle and anonymity steadily harder to maintain. 'It's getting a bit battered,' he told *IndieLondon* after the release of

3: REDEMPTION FROM THE LIMELIGHT IN PERDITION

The Jacket, John Maybury's psychological thriller with Keira Knightley and Adrien Brody. 'All I know is that I've tried to protect my privacy as long as possible and I will continue to do so because it's got fuck all to do with anybody. I mean this hasn't,' he vented. 'This is what I do and is part of what I do for a living. But the rest of it is nobody's business. The same as nobody's private life is anyone's business, even if you are in the public eye. There should be a clearly defined line and I don't think its brain surgery to try and figure that out. It's fairly simple. There's privacy and then there's public life. If you choose to be in the public life, then maybe you open yourself up to all sorts of rubbish. But if you don't then I think that should be respected.'

Also out was *Archangel,* a TV adaptation of Robert Harris's best-seller about an Oxford historian's investigation in the secrets around Stalin's death. In the second half of 2005 Daniel spent three months filming *Munich,* Spielberg's story of the Black September aftermath, when a team of Mossad agents set out to revenge the death of 11 Israeli Olympic athletes at the hand of a Palestinian terrorist group in 1972.

Shortly after filming wrapped in September, another story about Daniel's personal life hit the headlines. After the Kate Moss affair so badly bruised his sense of privacy a year earlier, it was particularly painful. This time, it involved his *Layer Cake* co-star, Sienna Miller, with whom he was lured into consuming his on-screen relationship in real life.

Sienna had been engaged to Jude Law since the new year, but all was not well. Jude himself had recently had an unfortunately brush with the tabloids when it transpired he had slept with his children's nanny, a young woman by the name of Daisy Wright. Whilst Jude had hoped to work things out with Sienna, she was furious and evidently decided to seek revenge by sleeping with one of his best friends.

The so-called Primrose Hill Set is renowned for its relaxed attitudes to partnerships and espousal of free love, and the group's antics have paid the rent of magazine and tabloid journalists for years. Jude himself had been in the headlines a year earlier, when it was reported that he had shared his bed with Kate Moss at the same time as ex-wife Sadie Frost. He had also begun an affair with Pearl Lowe, Supergrass drummer Danny Goffey's girlfriend, after exchanging partners while he was still married to Frost.

'The problem with Jude is that he finds the bohemian lifestyle of the Primrose Hill set tremendously exciting, but he's not very good at it,' said a friend. 'He got far too attached to Pearl and developed a bit of an obsession with her. The way he behaved was crushingly uncool. And with Kate he was a rabbit trapped in the headlights. For all his fame and money, Jude is basically a bit of a nerd, and that is a cardinal sin in Primrose Hill. When Sienna ended up sleeping with Daniel Craig behind his back, everyone just laughed. There certainly wasn't a great deal of sympathy for him.'

Jude Law and Sienna Miller on the set of *Alfie* (2004)

When Jude found out about Sienna's affair he threw her out of the house they shared in London. 'Jude is devastated and depressed; he is not in a good state right now,' a source told the *Daily Mail*. 'Sienna's friendship with Daniel has always made Jude nervous but he cannot believe that she has done this to him – especially as she always goes on about the importance of monogamy.' As they say, what goes around comes around: no one could say Jude didn't have it coming.

When Jude found out about the affair, he also phoned Daniel to berate him for this betrayal. 'A friend told Jude about the fling last week and when he confronted Sienna she admitted it was true. He is just so low and feels as though he has bent over backwards trying to win her trust and this is how she has repaid him. Ever since he confessed to his affair with Daisy, he has done everything he can to make it up to Sienna. But since they got back together, she has treated him so badly – going out all the time and not telling him where she's been going. Now this.'

'Sienna and Daniel became exceptionally close during the filming of *Layer Cake*,' the friend added. 'When Jude and Sienna subsequently got together, Daniel and Sienna's relationship deteriorated badly, to the extent that they stopped speaking. Sienna only recently confessed just how close she and Daniel once were – much to Jude's upset. Then, after she and Jude split up she arranged to meet Daniel and even cooked him an amazingly romantic Thai meal, complete with an exotic Thai massage. When Jude found out about the meal, he was livid – because Sienna had done exactly the same thing for him only weeks earlier!'

For a week or two Daniel and Sienna were occasionally spotted out around town, though again used the separate taxis trick to throw the paparazzi off the scent. 'Sienna is not at all contrite about her affair with Daniel and isn't upset about the split,' another source told the *Daily Mail*. After finding out about them, Jude had gone to Spain to recover and hide from the press. 'She even told Jude, "You and I are one of a kind," because she believes neither of them is capable of fidelity.'

Although Jude and Sienna's relationship was now in tatters – they would eventually break up for good in 2006 – Daniel was not so unfortunate. Just before news

3: REDEMPTION FROM THE LIMELIGHT IN PERDITION

of the 'Burnt Sienna' story and her subsequent revenge fling with Daniel came to light, he had been linked with film producer Satsuki Mitchell, who had also worked on *The Jacket*. Their relationship, despite being in its early stages, was not wrecked. Sienna went on her way – back to sporadically torment Jude for another year – and Daniel went on his.

'Daniel finds his lifestyle very exciting at the moment because being a heartthrob is a new experience for him,' one of his friends related to the *Daily Mail*. 'He was a bit of a geek at school and wasn't very popular with the girls. So to find that he suddenly has this rugged appeal is an amazing thing. He certainly won't be planning to settle down with Sienna, though. Firstly, because he loves his freedom. Secondly, and more significantly, he is a bit of a snob when it comes to choosing girlfriends. Girls like Sienna are fine for a bit of fun, but for long-term relationships he likes serious actresses – someone whom he considers his intellectual equal.' Satsuki certainly fits that particular billing.

'He's still mates with Jude,' claimed the source. 'Everyone accepted that it was just Sienna getting her own back and it wasn't worth two mates falling out over. In any case, it's not really regarded as a big deal in the Primrose Hill set if you sleep around. It's all quite normal. And after all, they knew he was a hit with the ladies because of what happened with Kate.'

Eva Green, Daniel Craig and Caterina Murino: *Casino Royale* film premiere, Paris, 17 November 2006

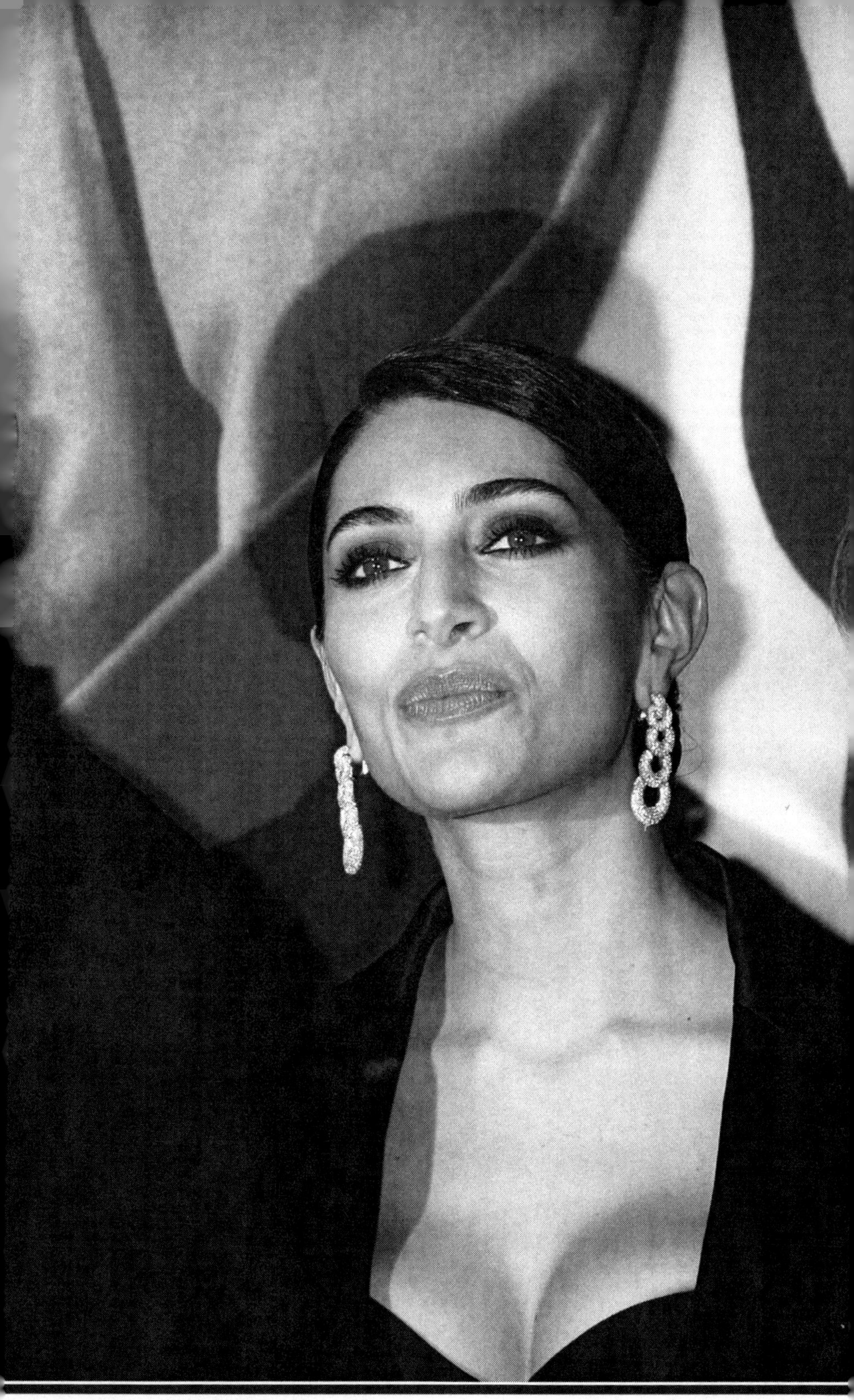

CASINO ROYALE
CASINO
ROYALE
ALBERT R. BROCCOLI'S EON PRODUCTIONS PRESENTS DANIEL CRAIG AS IAN FLEMING'S JAMES BOND 007 IN "CASINO ROYALE" EVA GREEN MADS MIKKELSEN
WITH JEFFREY WRIGHT AND JUDI DENCH AS "M"
DIRECTED BY MARTIN CAMPBELL
FEATURING "YOU KNOW MY NAME" PERFORMED BY CHRIS CORNELL
COLUMBIA PICTURES
CasinoRoyaleMovie.com
NOVEMBER 17

CH 4

JAMES BOND or JAMES BLAND?

At the same time the Sienna story came to light, Daniel was signing a contract for the biggest role of his life. The adverse publicity from the hard-core Bond fans hadn't dented his popularity enough to hold the casting directors back and he had been confirmed to start work on the 21st Bond film, *Casino Royale,* in January 2006. Hand-in-hand with the promotional interviews he did for that came plenty of awkward questions about his personal life. 'I'm not going to talk to you about press speculation,' he told one reporter. 'That's why they call me James Bland, because they asked me about that at that first press conference and I wouldn't answer, and I'm certainly not going to start now. So you can call me James Bland if you like.'

Although he now realised that promotional interviews for his films were unavoidable, nothing had changed about his decision to avoid lifestyle press – if anything, he was even keener to maintain his silence after the Moss/Miller stories. 'I'd never talk about a previous relationship even if I wasn't with somebody famous and so I think the same rule has to be applied. The only reason why I'd ever talk about that would be for my own advantage and that's really bad news. That's as low as you can go as far as I'm concerned.'

Despite the fact that he had already been offered the part of Bond, Daniel hadn't immediately put the rest of his acting career on hold, coolly refusing to tie himself down and accept the part before he knew more about it. 'They told me they were doing *Casino Royale,* that they wanted to take it back and they wanted a more emotional Bond but there wasn't a script. I was very honoured to be asked but I just walked away and said "I will read the script when you get it." Then I got on with my life and went to shoot *Munich*.'

He spoke about the process of casting on Virgin Radio later in 2005. Producer Barbara Broccoli had contacted him at the beginning of the year to try out for the part. 'I hadn't many ambitions to do this but Barbara gave me a call and said, "Please come and say hello." I thought, this is a bit of a giggle. I got a copy of the book and I was reading it but I'd ripped the front cover off it because going on the Tube reading it was a bit kind of...'

'I got off the Tube, finished the last page and threw it in the bin and went "Well, that was alright", walked into the offices and sat down with them. They said they wanted to go ahead with this and I just wish I kept that book.' Because the last Bond film, *Die Another Day*, had been such a critical disaster – relying on CGI, special effects and gadgets to the detriment of plot and characterisation – he was keen to see the script before he signed on the dotted line.

'I read it and I loved it,' he said. 'It engaged me, it made me laugh, it did all the things you want. So then I thought, I've got to throw myself into this.' Daniel was initially sceptical, thinking it would be better not to touch this project. Despite the fact that Bond is such an iconic character, few of his actors have had much in the way of careers before they took the role; he, on the other hand, had a substantial CV and reputation that could be adversely affected by selling out to the franchise if the script was terrible. Creative input from Paul Haggis, writer of *Million Dollar Baby* and *Crash*, finally convinced him.

'Paul Haggis had sprinkled his magic dust on it. I was honestly wanting to dislike it. It would have been an easy decision. I could have said, "That's very nice. Good luck with it." But it was too much. I sweated when I read the script. I thought, this is a great story, probably because it adhered to the book quite closely, and I just thought, "You've got to be really silly not to have a think about this."'

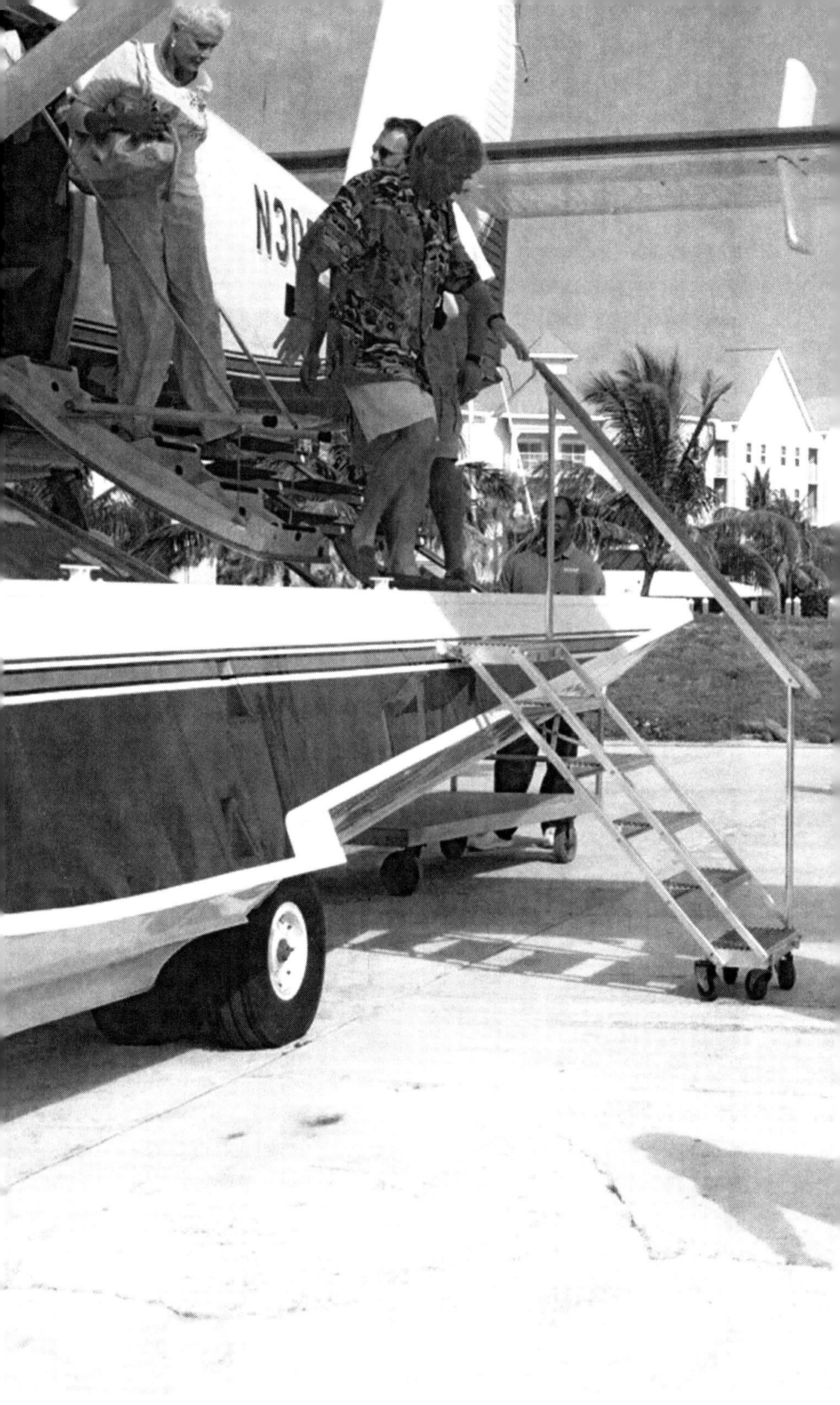

Daniel Craig as James Bond, *Casino Royale*, 2006

'I made pro and con lists. Every time the pros outdid the cons. The cons were like: you're going to get typecast. Which is a high-class problem to have... I kind of feel that if you look at the track record of most Bonds – I mean Sean Connery obviously defined the part, and even he struggled for a while to get rid of the mantle. That's the pitfall and it could happen to me. I've been working so hard, for however long it is I've been doing this, to try and stick to doing stuff I totally believe in and that would be wiped out. I thought, God, this is all right: I'm doing what I want to do. And that was a huge weight off my shoulders.'

'You might not be able to do other stuff,' he continued, 'to which I replied, "Who says?"' A meeting with Pierce Brosnan helped allay his fears over this last point; whilst contracted to star in the Bond films, Brosnan also acted in other successful films, including *The Thomas Crown Affair* remake. 'He said, "Go for it. It's a ride."'

Daniel spoke about his reaction when he finally heard he'd got the part for sure. 'I was shopping, and I dropped what I was carrying. I went straight to the alcohol section and got myself a bottle of vodka and a bottle of vermouth and went back and made myself a Martini – or two.' In October 2005, he signed a contract for three films. The first, *Casino Royale,* was to be released in November, 2006.

Infamous
The knowledge that he would be playing the next Bond

coloured his career from that moment on. Although there was no harm in terms of publicity, it did mean that the films released in the run up to *Casino Royale* would – rather unfairly – be judged increasingly on whether they showed him in a favourable light as Fleming's MI6 agent.

Infamous was the story of Truman Capote's relationship with two murderers as he researched the classic 'non-fiction novel' *In Cold Blood*. Daniel was playing Perry Smith; Toby Jones starred as Capote. Despite a stunning cast – Gwyneth Paltrow, Sigourney Weaver and Sandra Bullock also featured – what drew most attention was the bisexual Perry's growing attachment to Capote. This included a scene in which the two kiss, something that raised Daniel's profile even further in the gay community. ('I'm not knocking it,' he recently said. 'If I am a gay icon, that's fantastic.')

'The implications of falling in love with Daniel Craig!' Jones mused in an interview with the *Chicago Sun-Times*. 'He wasn't Bond when we did it, so I was only dimly aware of that whole thing during filming. It wasn't hard to kiss him.' Jones said he found Daniel 'physically scary' but great fun to work with, describing the kiss as 'slightly abrasive, ultimately rewarding… and neither of us is gay,' he quickly clarified. On a night out during the filming of *Casino Royale,* Daniel was amazed to find himself surrounded by gay admirers. 'I was out recently and all these gay guys were all over me like a rash, but they never ask about the Bond plot!' Secure in his own heterosexuality, Craig never bothers to deny that he is gay.

Infamous (2006). Toby Jones and Daniel Craig.

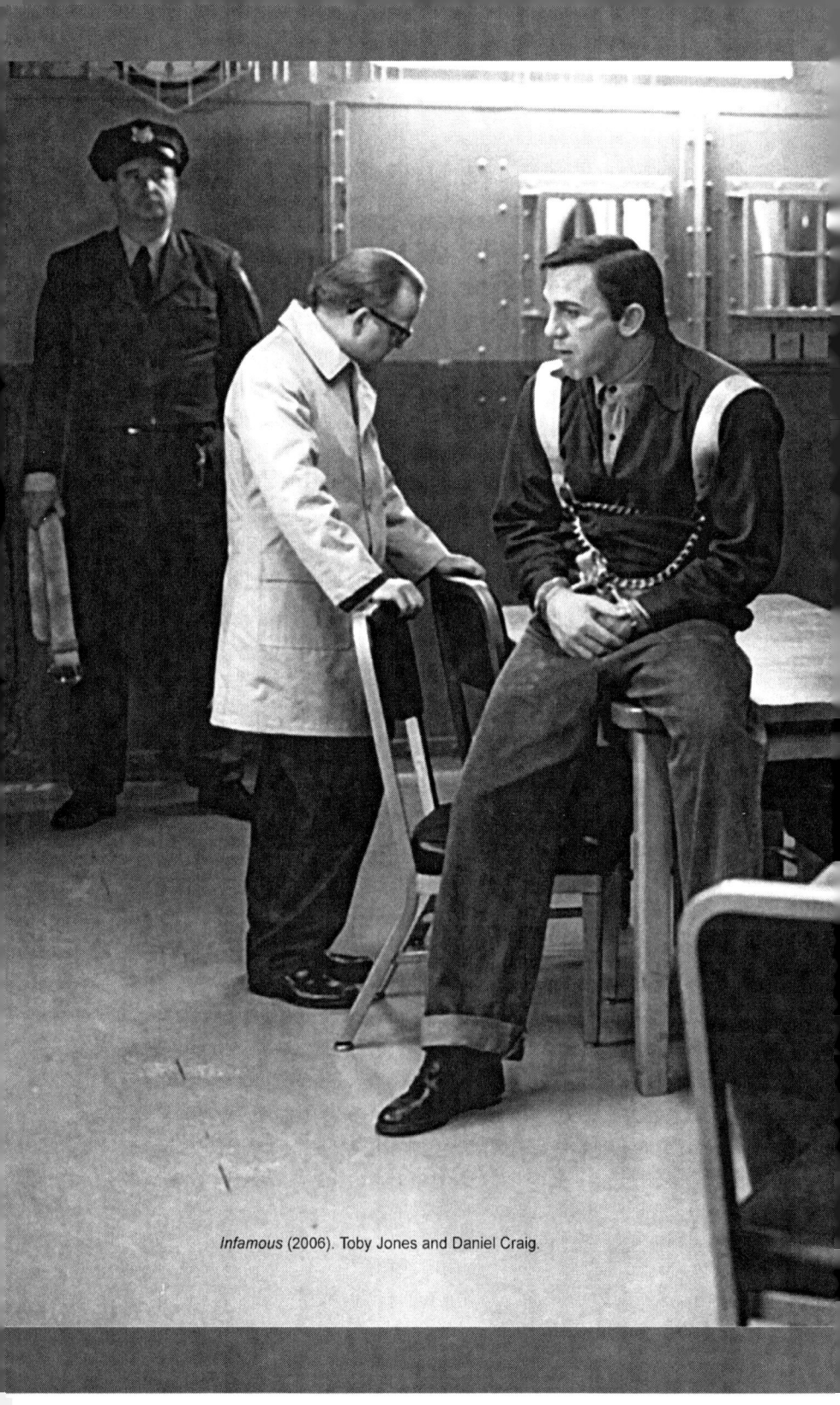

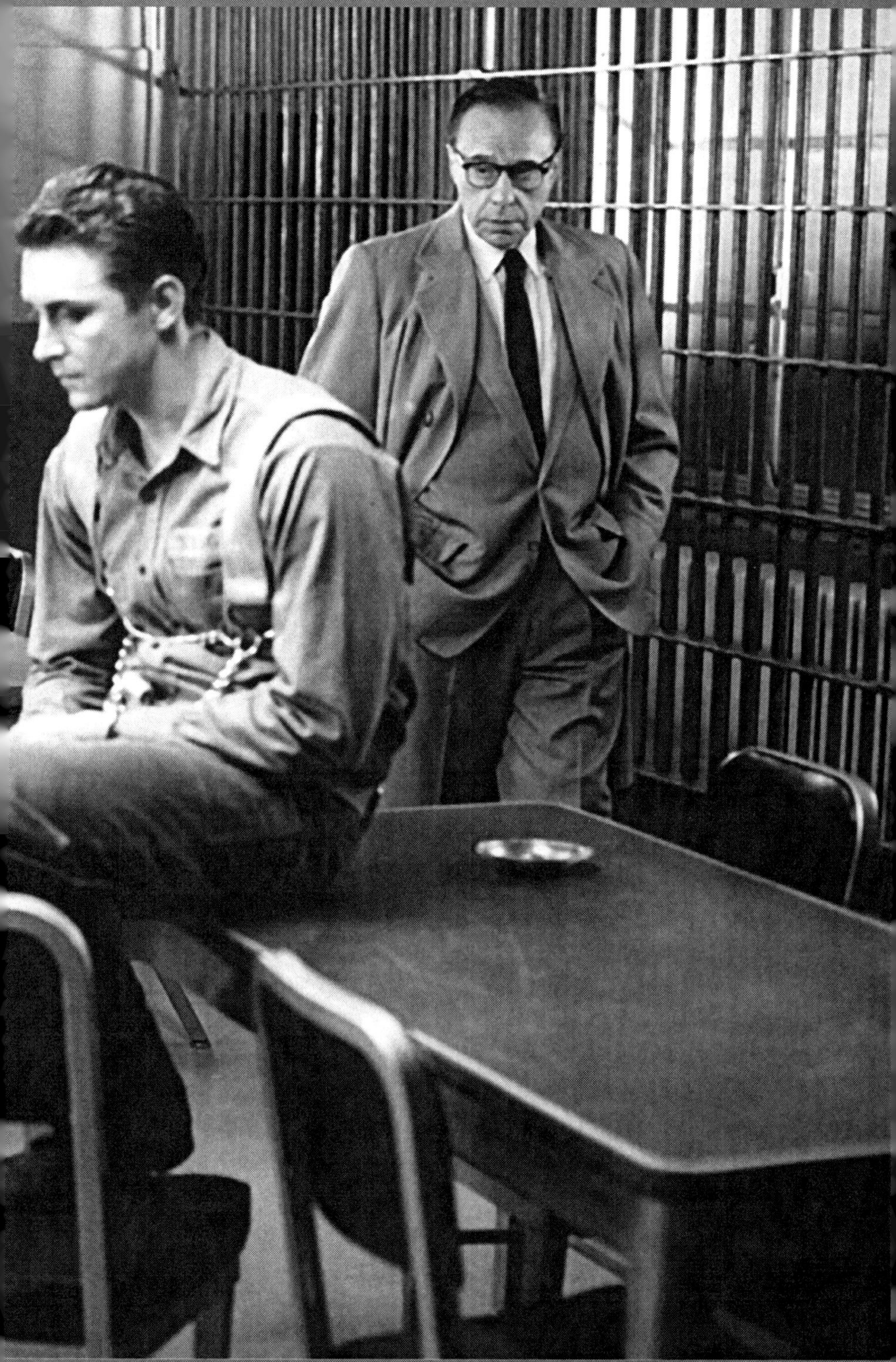

Predictably, rumours subsequently abounded that he was leaning on his producers to include full-frontal nudity and a gay scene in the next Bond film. Instead what Barbara Broccoli gave us was the male rig version of the camel toe shot of Ursula Andress in the first Bond movie, *Dr No*, coming out of the sea in her crevice-hugging bikini. Craig is on record that the gun in his trunks was not all his but, if he had a silencer fitted, it certainly gagged the critics, kept the gay and female viewers happy, the producers ecstatic and La Perla, the trunks manufacturors , walking on water all the way to the bank.

Looking the Part

Right at the beginning Daniel decided that, if he was going to do this, he was going to do it properly. 'If Bond should at some point take his shirt off, we should feel that he's physically imposing, that he's done the things he's supposed to have done, like being a commander in the Navy.' He threw himself into a harsh training programme, in order both to look the part and to be able to deal with the action scenes the film would involve. 'I did a lot of weights. I wanted to bulk up quickly and so I had a lot of high protein diets and that sort of thing.' The result was striking.

'He's the most rugged Bond the franchise has ever seen,' Zoe Williams wrote in *The Guardian*. 'Hunky Daniel Craig put his body through a punishing fitness regime to play James Bond,' Philip Boucher wrote admiringly in *The Daily Star*. 'And the result is a rippling torso most fellas would kill for.'

4: JAMES BOND or JAMES BLAND?

Daniel showed his new body off in the beach scene which more than a few critics spotted was a reprise of Ursula *Undress* emerging from the water in *Dr No*. The shot was timed to coincide with the high point in his physical training. 'By the time we got to the Bahamas, we kind of peaked, and that's where you see me walking out of the water. That was the peak of it, but we then kind of balanced it out,' he said. One critic described the scene as '...so scorchingly hot I feel embarrassed watching it, even when alone.'

'The trunks were my choice,' Daniel admitted. 'We sat with ten pairs on the table and discussed them at length. I mean, I just don't think Bond should wear Bermuda shorts. It's just not right. Anyway, the ones I chose aren't that skimpy. I mean, they're not Speedos. That would have been wrong.'

Whilst male and female fans would admire his toned physique in the finished product – he gained 20 pounds of muscle during shooting – Daniel was constantly confronted by the anti-Craig lobby, who spread rumours about his incompetence and even organised a boycott when the film was released. 'I didn't expect this backlash,' he said. 'You take it in, you can't help it. I've been trying to give 110 per cent since the beginning but after all the fuss, maybe I started giving 115 per cent.'

'They hate me,' he said in an interview with *Entertainment Weekly* magazine. 'They don't think I'm right for the role. It's as simple as that. They're passionate about it, which I understand, but I do wish they'd reserve judgement. If I went onto the Internet and started looking at what some people were saying about me – which, sadly, I have done – it would drive me insane.'

One of the most persistent pieces of propaganda was that Daniel didn't know how to drive a manual car, being used to automatics, and that Bond was therefore unable to pull away smoothly in his new Aston Martin. 'Of course I can drive a manual car,' he hit back. It was a sign of his unease that he actually engaged with the press on the issue – usually he would not bother. 'I flogged the arse out of an Aston Martin DBS around Jeremy Clarkson's *Top Gear* track. And in the film I got the car up to 170mph. When I braked, we had those brakes just fucking glowing. Will that do?' He explained the origins of the misinformation. 'Sorry, but most posh cars are automatic. I think someone leaked that I drove one which gets changed to, "Ha, ha! You can't change gear!"'

He was accused of getting seasick on a boat journey across the Thames to a press conference – something that would never happen to Bond. 'You know, normally I wouldn't answer these questions, but fuck it, no I didn't get queasy on that boat,' he replied. Then there was the occurrence during filming a fight scene where he is said to have lost two teeth. Despite the fact that this event was frequently quoted in the press and on the internet, it was another exaggeration; in reality, just a crown had come loose. 'Some of the stuff that's been said is as close to playground taunts as you're going to get. "You've got big ears"... fucking hell! But it's not right. Ask anyone who's been bullied... it hurts. There's a part of me that would love to turn around and shove it up their arse.'

Comments he'd made in the past also came back to haunt him. After *Layer Cake*, for example, he had defended himself against accusations that the film glorified crime and violence in a way that hardly added up to the man's man image required for a James Bond.

It's a horrible contradiction. I hate handguns. Handguns are used to shoot people and as long as they are around, people will shoot each other. That's a simple fact. I've seen a bullet wound and it was a mess. Bullets have a nasty habit of finding their target and that's what's scary about them.

People forget that. I feel we glamorise it, but I think you kind of have to have a bit of that. I think we have to scare people, so that when guns are fired, people jump.

Daniel's take on guns is definitively Freudian. 'They are big cocks basically. You get guys on screen and they're getting their cocks out and that I find boring. If you're going to use them in movies, you've got to find a way of using them that's gonna make you think about it.' Bond purists were unimpressed but there is no denying that in *Casino Royale* Bond has a very big gun. And there is no doubt, too, that the ladies are of the opinion that he knows how to use it.

At one stage Tim Craig, Daniel's father, even waded in with a testimonial to his son's gungho attitude to guns (inevitably prompting some critics to assert that he needed his dad to fight for him). 'It is all cobblers,' he told the *Sunday Mirror*. 'Daniel's a hard lad – you wouldn't want to meet him in a dark street. Is he a wimp? No, I wouldn't like to call him that to his face. As for the idea he doesn't like guns – when he was younger he would play with a toy gun like any other boy.' With supporters like this who needs detractors?

DANIEL CRAIG

James Bond: Casino Royale, 2006

'I was affected by it – of course I was,' Daniel later said. 'What bothered me was that I was being criticized before I had done the work. I wasn't going to get into an argument with these people, so my only response was, "See the movie and then you have the right to criticize, but first see what I am trying to do." It strengthened my resolve. I was hurt by it, but it just made me try harder. The pressure was there. I know a lot of people feel very passionate about the Bond movies, but so do I, so I just got on with it.'

Whilst many were heckling him for his perceived shortcomings, others were just as vocal in stating their support. Four previous Bond actors – Connery, Dalton, Moore and Brosnan – went on record to praise the casting decision. 'I'm looking forward to it like we're all looking forward to it,' Brosnan told the *Globe and Mail*. 'Daniel Craig is a great actor and he's going to do a fantastic job.'

Connery's endorsement was particularly encouraging for Daniel. 'He did something extraordinary with that role,' he said. 'He was bad, sexy, animalistic and stylish, and it is because of him I am here today. I wanted Sean Connery's approval and he sent me messages of support, which meant a lot to me.'

The producers were impressed enough with his work to sign him for the next film, with an option on a third. What is interesting is that his pay was £1.5 million for *Casino Royale* – a huge sum of money, but small beer given previous fees. Brosnan was apparently dropped after demanding no less than £22 million for his next appearance. Daniel is said to have negotiated £3 and £4 million for his second and third Bond films. 'Daniel is very much a poor man's 007,' one critic wrote. 'He's facing an uphill battle to win over Bond fans before *Casino Royale* is even released, and it looks like producers got him slightly on the cheap.'

Audience figures proved that Craig won the uphill battle. As for him being a cheap deal! Daniel is said to be 'happy with the arrangements,' even speculating about what he will do with the cash from future movies. 'I'd love to get into buying art, though I haven't started making enough money yet,' he suggested.

Filming *Casino Royale* was the most physically demanding film he had ever made. But alongside the stunt spectaculars and action sequences, Craig was keen to give some depth to Bond. Previous 007 films had become light on characterisation, portraying the hero as a two-dimensional near-superman who is always going to coolly upstage the baddies and always with a smart Alec quip.

This one, which started at the beginning of Bond's career as a 00-agent, needed someone more human, more fallible. It meant showing emotion and vulnerability as well as fear and anger, as the spy is gradually shaped into the form we are now familiar with. With his background across such an extensive range of stage and movie projects, Daniel was ideal for this aspect of the part.

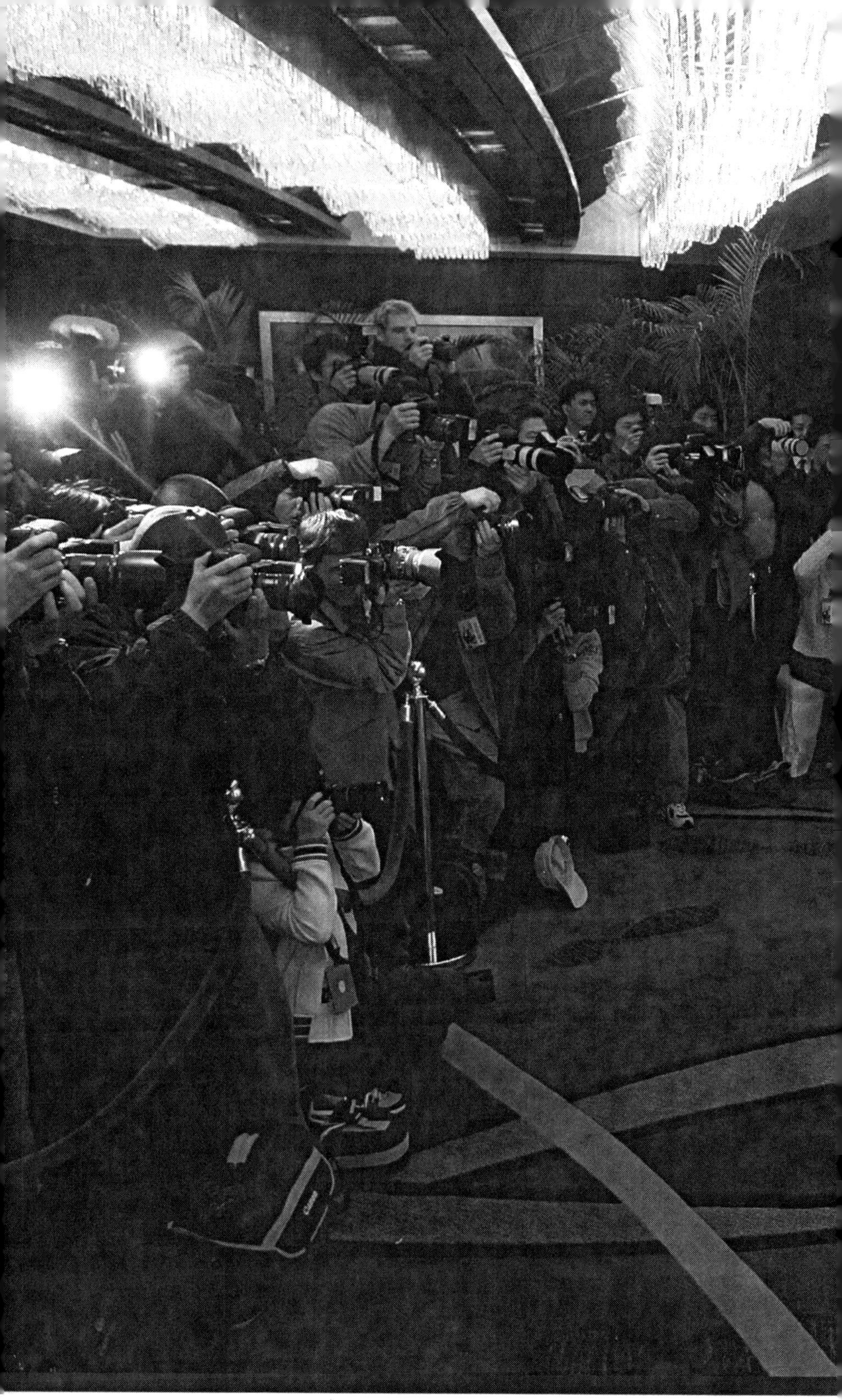

Casino Royale film press conference in Beijing, 29 January 2007.

'I just wanted to see him make a few mistakes. I want to make the audience believe that it's all going to go wrong and then when it goes right it's much more exciting,' he said. 'What I tried to achieve was just making a movie people will want to go and see, and I think we have made a great movie. One of the things I was criticized for was that I looked like a bad guy, but I was happy with that because I think true good guys have to step into the dark side to do their job. I wanted people to question Bond's morals and his judgment.'

For all the rumours that he was too much of a wimp to be convincing, *Casino Royale* is actually by Bond film standards very violent. In order to make sure it looked as realistic as possible, Daniel insisted on doing as much of his own stunt work as the producers allowed. 'I wanted to do as much of the action scenes as I could, so that the audience can see it's me and it's real. I feel like I became a sportsman of sorts, and that meant acquiring injuries and carrying on and bashing through to the next level of pain,' he said. 'Although the stunt team did fantastic work to make sure that everything was as safe as possible, if you don't get bruised playing Bond, you're not doing it properly. I had black eyes, I had cuts, I was bruised, I had muscle strains, and I took a lot of painkillers. But it was part of the job. As much as I was hurt, the stuntmen were in much more pain.'

'That's the thing with Bond, he bleeds, goes down and gets up again,' he told *GQ* magazine. 'There's a bathroom sequence that still makes me wince when I watch it. All my knuckles were split and my hands were in bandages after it. I had a fight double named Ben. I did the bits that hurt and he did the bits that really fucking hurt! The stunt boys were going through pain levels that I couldn't even imagine and still carrying on. Compressed spines, all sorts of things.'

This was the part of filming that his critics didn't report on. 'I got a cap knocked out, but that was the least of my problems,' he said, referring to the event that had been so badly exaggerated by his detractors. He pointed out rather painfully:

You have no idea of the fucking injuries I was picking up during that movie. But then the whole of Casino Royale was a painful experience. I was in pain throughout the whole movie. But you can't show pain.

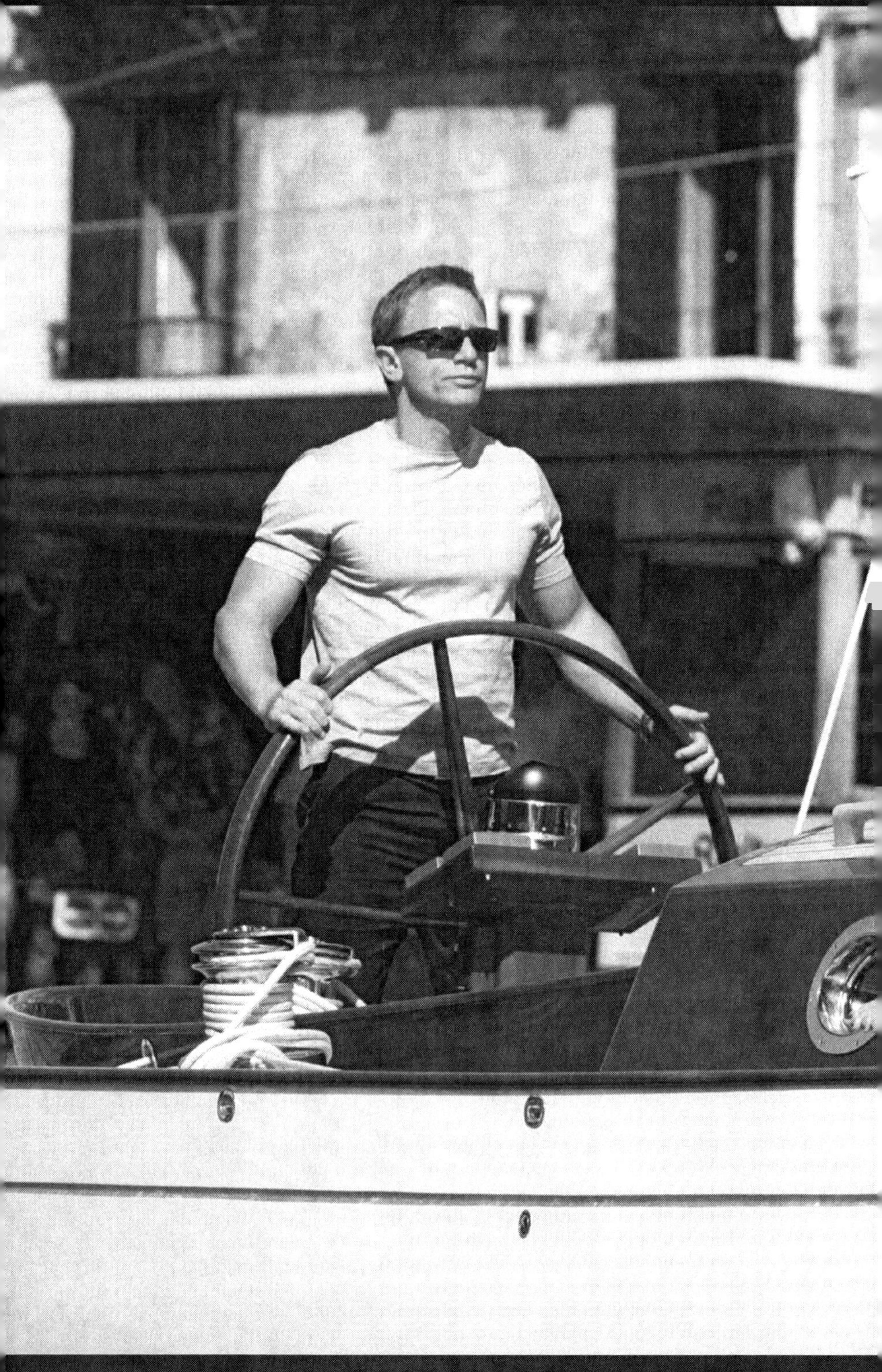

Casino Royale film set: Venice, 7 June 2007.

'Nothing that you see in the movie, stunt-wise, is not happening,' he continued. 'It's all happening. And if it's not me doing, it's someone else doing it, and they're getting hurt. You also find out what it's like falling down a flight of stairs. It feels like you're falling down a fucking flight of stairs. And that's what we wanted to feel. We wanted to feel the pain, the pain in it.'

One scene in particular will haunt him (and male cinema-goers the world over) for years to come. The torture sequence is lifted directly from Fleming's original novel, except the film uses a piece of knotted rope not, as in the book, a carpet beater. 'The bad guy takes the bottom out of a chair. I'm sat in it naked and supposedly my nuts are hanging down there, although I think in that situation they would kind of go north,' Daniel said to *GQ*. 'The bad guy gets a spliced piece of rope and he swings it under the chair and does me with it. It all has fibreglass protection but it did crack at one point and we stopped filming quite rapidly and I ran over the other side of the room. Woah!'

'Every day you pick up an injury and you're battered and bruised. If you're not physically fit then it's difficult to get through. I'm a Bond fan. If I go and see a Bond movie there are certain things I think should be in it. And they're there. We've got them in spades. Nobody knows more than I do how important this is, and it's my job to get it right.' Stunts and sadism is one thing we expect from a Bond movie.

The girls are another. French actress Eva Green was

chosen to play Vesper Lynd, the British treasury official who becomes his missionary accomplice. Green spoke of how the two of them immediately formed a good rapport. 'Daniel is amazingly hypnotic, he's magnetic... he's a true gentleman,' she told Sofeminine.co.uk. He has a real physical presence and a certain amount of brutality which I think is so sexy, it's kind of dangerous. He's a real man! I think that's why he's such a credible Bond in all the different situations in the film. He's really sexy and he has the greatest sense of humour, he doesn't miss a thing! We got on straight away.'

Naturally, there were the obligatory sex scenes, though Daniel typically downplayed them: 'You can never feel comfortable in those situations. You're in a sex scene where there are ten people in the room you don't know that well. So you're not exactly feeling sexy unless you get a kick out of that, which some people do. But I don't.' Eva was more positive about the experience. 'I surprised myself because it was not so hard, you know? I stopped being self-conscious and questioning myself. I wanted to be good in every scene.'

As a relative unknown, she had even more to prove than Daniel. Having been directed by *Bernardo Bertolucci* in her first film, *The Dreamers,* in 2003, she fortunately had a head start on filming love scenes. 'When we were making love on the floor he was directing us like, how do you say chef d'orchestre? A conductor. You know, like: "Okay, okay. Orgasm. And then *ahhhh*. There we are." So you don't think. You do it.' Eva did not elaborate on how she does do it but, as she doesn't think, it could hardly be mind over vaginal matter.

After *Casino Royale* wrapped, Daniel was immediately thrown into a hectic schedule of promotion. 'We went straight into long-lead press, a junket for a week, where I actually had to go talk about the movie just as we finished it,' he told *iF* magazine. 'And it was one of the most bizarre experiences because I hadn't given it any thought. I'd been just working. People were going "What's it like to be Bond?" And I didn't know. I still don't really know. And then we went on holiday. So it's kind of never stopped. As much as I went away on holiday, the phone was ringing every day and we were discussing stuff about how we were going to do this and how we're going to do that and what the next stage is. It's a full-time job.'

After the physically demanding work of filming, a break was definitely a welcome idea. 'I went on holiday and let myself go in lots of ways,' he told *iF* magazine. 'But that was just because we were in France and eating good food and drinking lots of wine. And I have kept up going to the gym, but not quite as intensely as I was doing it during the film.'

In his spare time, Daniel says he likes to do as little as possible. 'I like fishing, I like painting... I like painting fish,' he told *Movieweb*. 'I get away. I try to go somewhere. There are a couple of places, which I won't tell you about, that are very private and very nice. I don't see family from one month to the next, so I have to go back and reconnect and make sure they still like me. Do those sorts of things.'

Casino Royale had a $150 million budget and the producers were pinning their hopes on Daniel to revive a tired franchise that looked like it was reaching the end of its days: expectations were high. When the film was released, most sceptics were instantly silenced by the finished work: the movie was heralded as a blinding triumph by the public and critics alike. Craig is definitely not James Bland.

'There's one whopper of a reason why *Casino Royale* is the hippest, highest-octane Bond film in ages, and his name is Daniel Craig,' wrote Peter Travers of *Rolling Stones*. 'This rugged, jug-eared Brit, whose irregular features improbably radiate a megawatt star charisma, gets the last laugh on the Internet buzz killers who've been ragging on him at craignotbond.com for being blond and blue-eyed and too short (five-eleven) for Bond duty. Not only is Craig, 38, the best Bond since Sean Connery, he's the first of the Bonds (great Scot Connery, one-shot George Lazenby, charmer Roger Moore, stuff-shirt Timothy Dalton and smoothie Pierce Brosnan) to lose the condescension and take the role seriously.'

It was a stunning turnaround for the man who had been belittled by the press in the previous months. Many of those who had slammed him before the movie was out now credited him for carrying the film and bringing an entirely new quality to the role. 'One aspect of the new

Bond that works from first minute to last is the most important one, and that is Craig's performance,' wrote the *LA Times*. '...the Bond franchise has always been fortunate in its choice of leading men, and Craig is one of their wisest picks yet.' 'Craig was inspired casting,' agreed *The Guardian's* Peter Bradshaw. 'He has effortless presence and lethal danger; he brings a serious actor's ability to a fundamentally unserious part; he brings out the playfulness and the absurdity, yet never sends it up. He's easily the best Bond since Sean Connery, and perhaps even...'

Casino Royale took over $40 million in the US on its opening weekend in November 2006, and £13 million in the UK – £4 million more than Brosnan's last, critically disastrous outing in *Die Another Day*. (Although it topped the UK box office, another dynamic was at work in the US that weekend, where *Happy Feet*, a film about dancing penguins, beat it to No. 1 .)

At the film's première Daniel was seen walking down the red carpet with Satsuki Mitchell. The pair had been dating for over a year, although he had rarely been seen out in public with her during that time. This was a rare occasion where he brought his private life into the public's scrutiny. After all, it was the finest hour of his career, so who could blame him? At the launch party he was seen cuddling her, in between posing with fans for photos and signing autographs. Asked who would be his ideal Bond girl, he indicated to Satsuki and said, 'This one here.' On one occasion, he even kissed her for the benefit of the cameras.

'We're together, and she's been experiencing this whole situation with me,' he said.

The première was attended by the Queen and Prince Philip, who shook hands with the film's stars before watching *Casino Royale*. 'This is pretty good, I can't explain how this feels,' Daniel said. 'It's fantastic. I'm just very excited. These sort of things happen once in a lifetime and I'm just trying to enjoy it.' Producer Barbara Broccoli was unreserved in her praise. 'He's a perfectionist, he's a brilliant actor, and he's a wonderful human being. And he's got a great bod!' she told *People*. It is a testament to his earlier work that she chose him for the role. 'I saw Daniel in *Our Friends in the North*,' she said to *The Times*. 'I saw him in *Elizabeth*, just walking down the hallway. I thought, "My God." He does have extraordinary presence. Just look at the body of work. He can be a character actor but he can also be a leading man. And a star. It's a pretty unique thing. He seemed the obvious choice. And he has surpassed our expectations.'

Some were suggesting he was the best and even sexiest Bond ever. 'I don't think about it,' said Daniel. 'I don't give it much thought.' Caterina Murino said that of all the past 007 actors, 'He is the sexy one, I'm sure.' Judi Dench (who reprised her 'M' role) was reserved in her opinion but only after making some surprisingly graphic remarks about him when she accidentally saw him naked in his trailer. 'I'm old enough to be his grandmother!', she simply commented. However, she did admit 'he was divine to work with.'

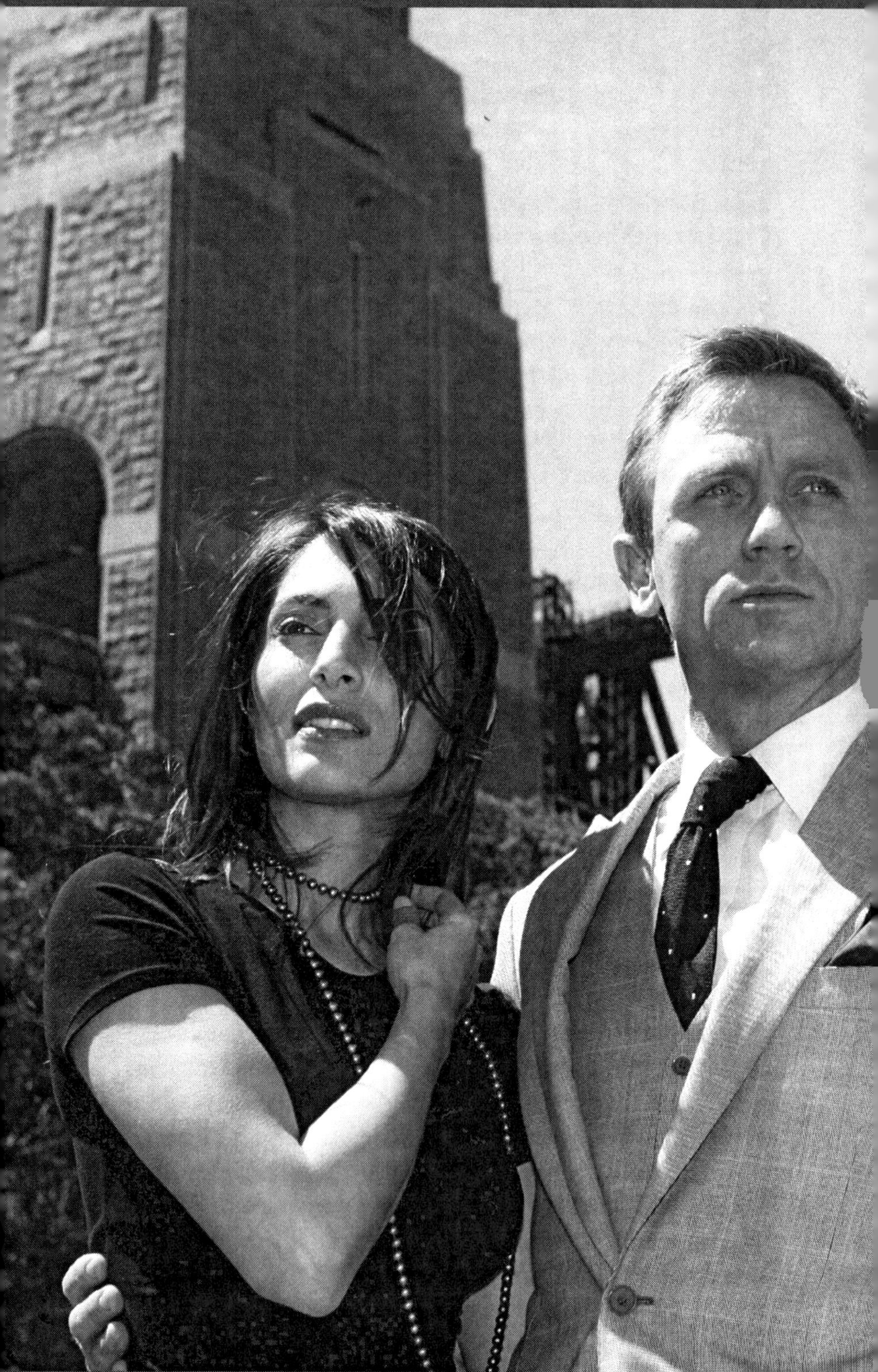

Daniel Craig and Caterina Murino at Park Hyatt Hotel, Sydney, Australia, 5 December 2006.

Casino Royale had been an incredible coup after the widespread sniping and criticism Daniel had suffered since being named for the role in February 2005. But it did leave him with the question of where he was going to go next – both professionally and personally.

For starters, it was clear that his private life was going to be a lot less easy. He had had a taste of that in the previous couple of years after his short-lived flings with Kate Moss and Sienna Miller. During the filming of *Casino Royale,* he related to *The Times,* the crew constantly had to deal with photographers sneaking onto the set to take secret pictures. On one occasion, he said, they were shooting scenes on a beach. 'We were filming and they discovered two guys buried up to their necks in the sand with cameras. They had been there all night.' He is now followed constantly by paparazzi and admits that, as far as his personal life is concerned, taking the part of James Bond has 'probably obliterated it.'

He has, however, spoken briefly about his relationship with Satsuki Mitchell. 'Any relationship needs a little love and care at least once a day,' he said. 'I don't want to get soppy about it, but you've got the put the time in. It doesn't matter who you are, you've got to keep putting it in.' Only time will tell whether he is really capable of that in the light of the upsurge in press interest, but Daniel has practised anonymity for over ten years now and has no intention of stopping. He names author JK Rowling as a great inspiration to him (Daniel is a keen *Harry Potter* fan) – someone who is hugely famous but who manages to keep her ego and lifestyle in check. 'She's kept her privacy,' he told *The Guardian*. 'I think she may have a child, but I don't know, which is good. Now she's using her money to fund things she believes in. But her charity is her own private thing, which I think is incredibly admirable.'

After the storm subsided, he had to re-engage and find out what shape his career was going to be in. He knew he had won the admiration of the big, commercial film-makers, but there was a real chance that other doors would have closed to him. 'Potentially, you cheapen your brand if you do this,' he said. 'Some people I talked to were against it. They said, "You may lose the chance to do the stuff you want to do."'

His concern was that independent film-makers would never touch him again – let alone retaining any hope of going back to theatre work. 'I hope it's going to be liberating,' he said optimistically. 'I'm not putting any negative spin on this because to be typecast as James Bond is a very high-class problem for an actor, and I'm certainly going to try to get as much out of it as I can. Of course I am always going to think about whether it is going to limit what I do. I plan for it not to, but if it does, I'll approach that problem when it comes.'

Of course, high-class problems tend to make their own solutions. After all, even if he does not draw the £22 million demanded by Brosman, £3 million a picture is no short straw. And having a bonanza Bond on his CV gives him a lot of bums-on-seats pull in the industry.

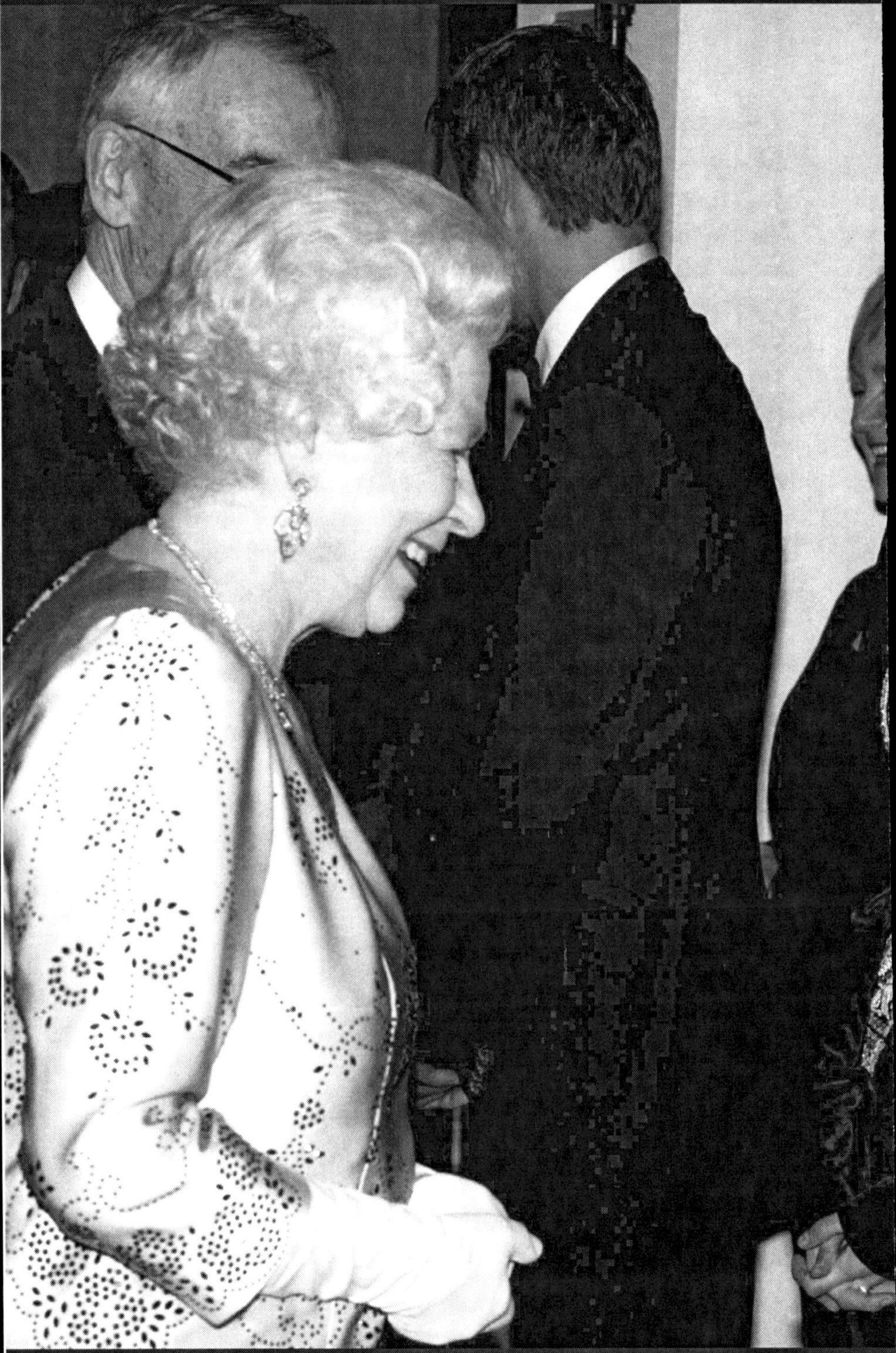

Casino Royale Premiere, 14 November 2006: Queen Elizabeth II meeting Eva Green and Daniel Craig

Bond 22, which is the working title of the direct sequel to *Casino Royale*, is to be released in November 2008. Before filming began on that, he had other projects to keep him busy. His first was the role of Lord Asriel in *His Dark Materials: The Golden Compass* (the first instalment of Philip Pullman's fantasy trilogy), starring opposite Nicole Kidman. It was hardly a step down after Bond; the film had a budget of $150 million. As it happened, one of his Bond predecessors, Timothy Dalton, had played the same part in a stage adaptation of the book in 2003.

The Invasion was also being finished – most of the film had been shot in 2005 but a few scenes were made in January 2007. He was again starring with Nicole Kidman, who related how Daniel had heard confirmation of his Bond part in the course of the earlier filming. 'In 24 hours he became a diva,' she joked to *W* magazine, before relenting. 'Oh, he didn't change at all. The thing about Daniel, and the reason I like working with him, is that he's an actor's actor.'

Daniel was pleased to work with Nicole, too, though for different reasons. He said in a classical Bondish turn of phrase:

She turns me on. Not in a sordid, horrible way... well, come to think of it...

4: JAMES BOND or JAMES BLAND?

Daniel's future doubtless holds more big-budget crowd-pleasers, but they are not what motivates him. Also on the horizon is *I, Lucifer*, a comic fantasy inspired by *Paradise Lost*. The premise of the film is that God has given Satan one last chance: he must live a blameless life as a human to achieve redemption. Satan, who has other ideas, negotiates a month in which to decide – which he intends to use for an all-out blitz of hedonism. Although the film was still a relatively large project – its budget is £14 million – Daniel was intrigued by the idea. He has also had some thoughts about further projects. One thing he has always hoped for is a role in Star Trek. 'I would love a stint in the TV show or in a film,' he said. 'It's been a secret ambition of mine for years.'

Ultimately, there is little question that Daniel will return to what he loves best – artistic, independent films that he finds interesting and fulfilling to act in. Alongside these there will doubtless be a string of blockbusters, but he sees these as a means to an end rather than an end in themselves. He now knows that any film he wants to do has a much better chance of financial backing.

Bond may have defined Daniel to a new generation of cinema-goers the world over, but one thing it won't do is restrict him. He knows where his priorities lie and isn't the kind of actor to sell out for the kind of paycheques that producers are now offering. 'Knowing him, I don't think he will change,' *Layer Cake* director's Matthew Vaughn told *The Independent*. 'I think he will be probably the first Bond who won't be eclipsed by it. He had such an amazing pedigree as an actor before he took it on, that there's no director who wouldn't still want to work with him after Bond.'

CONCLUSION

LIFE AFTER BOND: BLUE CHIP OR BONDAGE?

Director John Maybury, a close friend who worked with Daniel on *Love is the Devil* and *The Jacket*, is quite sure that he won't be tied down in bondage to 007. 'Bond can only empower him. He's the real deal. I think he can go anywhere he wants from here.'

It is quite clear where that is as he has already started going there. Craig is in for the long haul and wants to establish himself as an actor who can both carry films and play character parts. He wants in other words to call all the shots on his career and make it last all his life. He has served his apprenticeship and now he wants to move into Michael Caine territory, but with a difference. And the difference is where you get to the heart of the man. Craig wants to make some films that raise people's consciousness, show them lessons in how to live better lives. He is more than an actor: he is an artist.

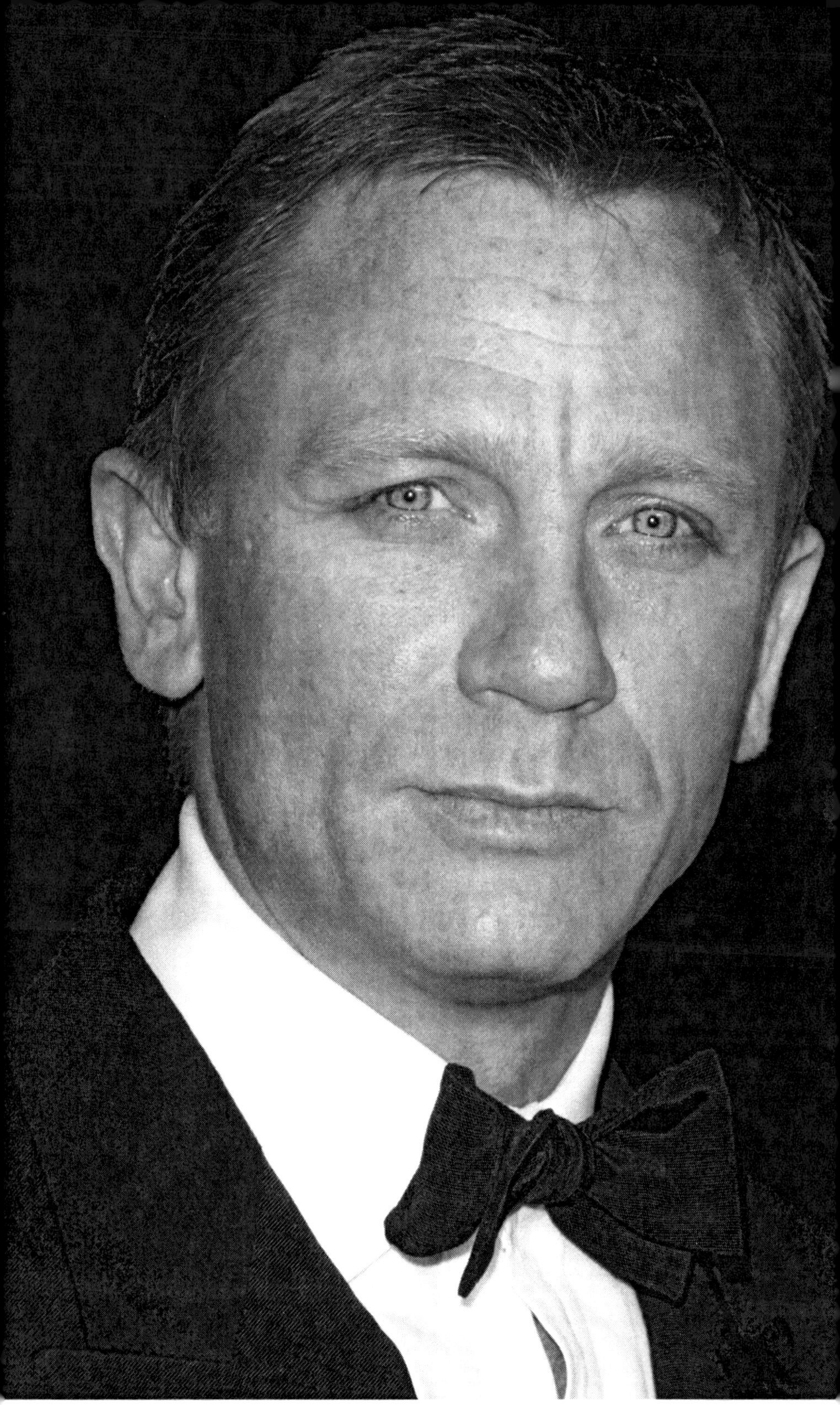

CONCLUSION

Bond has empowered him because *Royale* has proved to be the most profitable Bond movie to date. Not only that but *The Golden Compass*, the first part of Philip Pullman's *His Dark Materials* trilogy, in which Craig plays Lord Asriel, opened in December 2007 and is looking to be equally successful. In which case the backers will make Pullman's two sequels, which will mean Craig will be staring in two of the most lucrative franchises currently being scheduled. Incidentally, Craig has read the three Pullman books – 'twice'.

Towards the end of January 2008, the title of Bond 22 was revealed – *Quantum of Solace*, which is one of Ian Fleming's short stories first published in a woman's magazine in 1959. The term refers how one may make a precise measurement of the amount of comfort, fraternity and warmth need in a relationship for it to survive. Below that threshhold, Bond muses, 'You've got to get-away to save yourself... when the other person not only makes you feel totally insecure, but actually seems to want to destroy you.'

Producer Michael Wilson chose the title, which Craig conceded 'doesn't trip off the tongue.' Adding, 'But why should it?' Well, the short answer to that is it does help with publicity. The quirky title is clearly part of the policy of giving the new Bond more depth and inner turmoil. Bond has to come to terms with having his heart broken at the end of *Royale* and, according to Craig, *Quantum* is about him 'figuring a few things out' while indulging, of course, in the usual action heroics: it is lots of gadgets and stunts but with heart.

Meanwhile, in 2007, he made a low-budget film directed by Baillie Walsh, called *Flashbacks of a Fool*, which tracks the life of an ex-Hollywood actor's early years in England. Craig describes it as playing '...a movie star who goes through a huge change in his life, which maybe sounds a bit arrogant but the story is about growing up, what we learn when we're children and how we are formed as adults. We shot it in South Africa and it's a very simple story.' He admits that the success of *Royale* helped get the backing to make it.

He told Martyn Palmer of *The Times*: 'It's not going to be a huge money-spinner because it's not that kind of movie. But to be able to make films like this is important to me. I have to be all these other things now and acting starts dropping down the list, which is bizarre. You go...

'Hang on a minute, I just want to be an actor, I want to just turn up and do the gig.'

He is clearly still doing that, but more than as just a jobbing actor. In the autumn of 2007, he also made *Defiance*, which is the story of the four Bielski brothers who set up a resistance movement against the Nazis in the Belarussian forests. It's an unsung epic of survival, which was more about saving Jews from the holocaust than killing Nazis. Tuvia Bielski, whom Craig plays, never wavered in his conviction that it was more

CONCLUSION

important to save Jews than to kill Nazis. He also refused to turn away the weak or the old for the sake of the survival of the larger group and he would warn new arrivals to the forest, 'Life is difficult, we are in danger all the time, but if we perish, if we die, we die like human beings.' *Defiance* is the kind of movie that Bond has allowed Craig to make and the fact is, after only one Bond picture, he is making them.

Meanwhile, Craig is also rumoured to be marrying Satsuki Mitchell who accompanied him on much of the *Royale* publicity roller-coaster. He agrees that it is difficult keeping things together with her: 'It's a struggle, but I couldn't do it without having that closeness to somebody. Being on your own would be sad, sick and weird. I don't trust myself. I need that balance, it's crucially important. And we've been to some amazing places. I remember one night we were in this sky bar at the top of a beautiful hotel having a drink looking out over Beijing and just being blown away. You have to have someone to share this stuff with. We got a private viewing of the Sistine Chapel. A fantastic guy took us around and told us the history of all the paintings. How cool is that? I said to Sats, 'We have to remember this.'"

However, in November 2007, when Johnny Vaughn asked him about her on his London Capital radio show, he let rip. At the best of times, cheeky-chappie Vaughn is an intrusive pest and Craig had been on the Vodka Martinis the night before. Nonetheless, his reaction, even in anger, goes to the essence of the man:

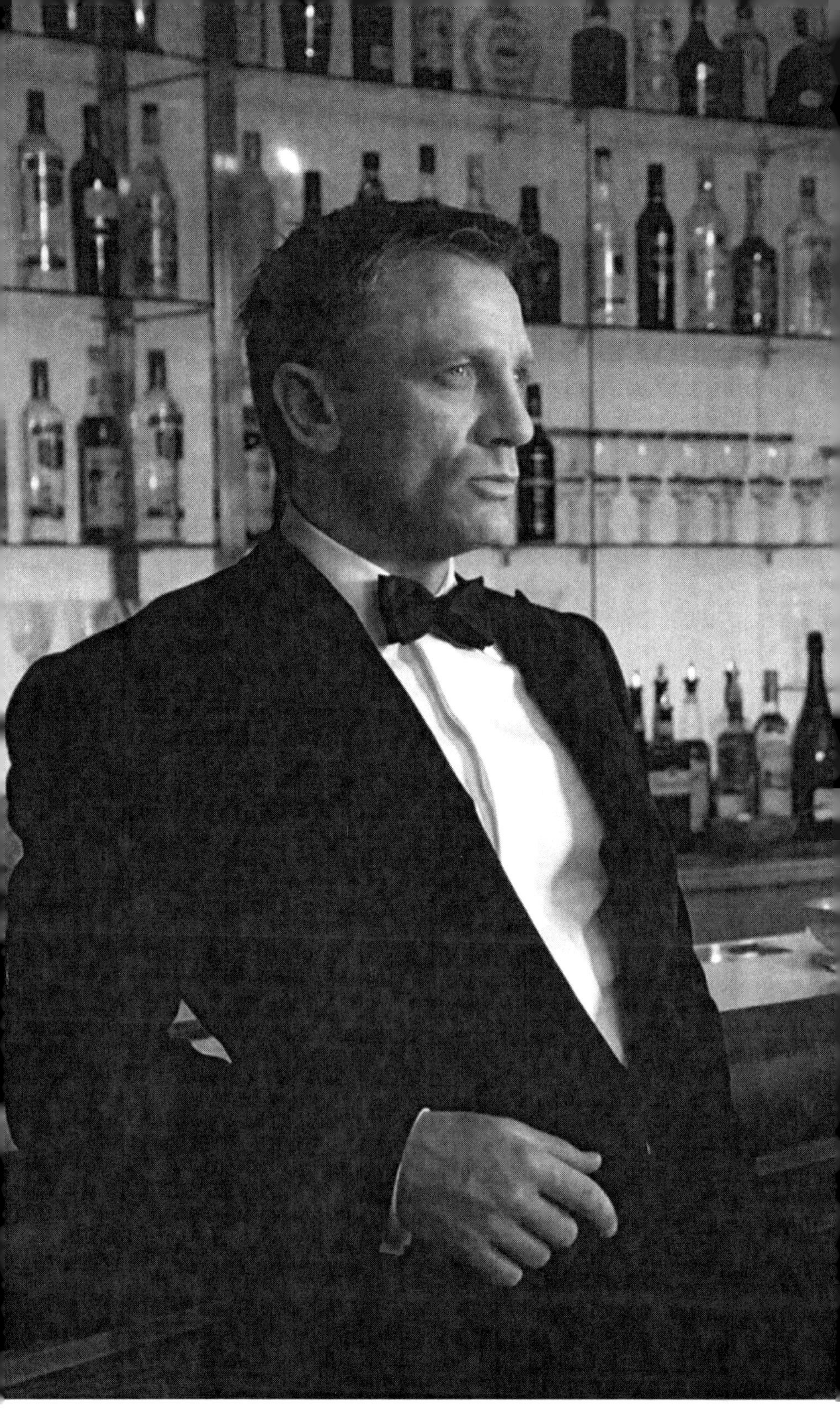

James Bond: *Casino Royale*, 2006.

'You know people who talk about themselves all the time? I think it's quite frankly fucking boring. I don't like talking about my personal life... It's wrong to sort of discuss my private life in public because it affects many other people I care about. It has nothing to do with *trying to get a better career.*' [author's italics]

He's conscious that doing Bond will intrude onto his private life. 'You know, if I'm up for it, fine. I have to keep hold of my sense of humour, because you can lose it very quickly and you start retreating into yourself; then you can't go anywhere unless you are with armed guards, and the whole thing becomes ridiculous. So you have to smile about these things.'

He went back to the gym for *Quantum* but he is not going for the ripped look of *Royale*. 'I was big for the last one, and it wasn't a mistake, it was a definite statement,' he claims. 'This guy, when he takes his shirt off, should look like he could kill someone. After it finished, I stopped training... relaxed for three months and ate what I wanted, and then it's hell because as soon as you get back in the gym, you have to work all that off, and it takes much longer than it does to put it on. Last time I did a lot of weights to bulk up. This time I'm going to do more boxing and more running. I need to be physically strong for Bond and, as much as I looked in great shape, I got a lot of injuries, probably due to the fact that I wasn't doing enough running and jumping. I won't look physically much different, but I won't be as *no-neck* as I was last time.'

CONCLUSION

However his preparation for *Quantum* has gone far beyond the physical. He's been hands-on with the director, Marc Forster, and the scriptwriter, Paul Haggis. Before they started shooting, Craig said of Forster whose *Kite Runner* he thinks is stunning: 'If you look at his current body of work that in itself makes me very excited, because they are such a diverse look at the world – I'd want us to have that. Marc is very solid and that for me is crucially important because this movie needs to jump on from *Casino Royale* and take it somewhere else. Marc is totally inspired.'

Paul Haggis, like Forster, is not someone you normally associate with Bond-style movies. A late-comer but a big hitter: his first two movies (*Million Dollar Baby* and then *Crash*, which he directed) grossed seven Oscars! He polished *Royale* and Craig has worked with him on the *Quantum* script. 'Paul has put another great script in. He is someone who can actually take on the story and the character and take it to a different place.' *Quantum* will raise the bar on the formula of the tired, old, tongue-in-cheek, special-effects Bond. It could well turn out to be a genuine on-the edge-of-your-seat thriller.

And Craig? An old acting mate recently asked him what's it like being an international star?' He answered, 'Well, I get to hang around with all the best women, drive the fastest cars, travel in speedboats and private jets, sleep in the best hotels and have beautiful women pursuing me from all over the world... and it's absolutely bloody awful!'

Printed in the United Kingdom
by Lightning Source UK Ltd.
128301UK00001B/13-69/P